SURVIVING
the STORMS *of*
LIFE

*Finding Hope and Healing
When Life Goes Wrong*

H. Norman Wright
Matt Woodley & Julie Woodley

Revell
a division of Baker Publishing Group
Grand Rapids, Michigan

© 2008 by H. Norman Wright, Matt Woodley, and Julie Woodley

Published by Revell
a division of Baker Publishing Group
P.O. Box 6287, Grand Rapids, MI 49516-6287
www.revellbooks.com

Printed in the United States of America

Library of Congress Cataloging-in-Publication Data
Wright, H. Norman.
    Surviving the storms of life : finding hope and healing when life goes wrong
/ H. Norman Wright, Matt Woodley, and Julie Woodley.
       p. cm.
    Includes bibliographical references.
    ISBN 978-0-8007-3235-6 (pbk.)
    1. Suffering—Religious aspects—Christianity. 2. Psychic trauma—Religious aspects—Christianity. I. Woodley, Matt. II. Woodley, Julie. III. Title.
BV4909.W75 2008
248.8′6—dc22
                                          2008008807

Mathew and Julie Woodley dedicate this book to their four beautiful children: Bonnie Joy (and her great husband, Trevor), Mathew, JonMichael, and Wesley. We are so blessed to call you our beloved children. It continually amazes us that God has ordained you to become such incredible people. You have been there through all of your parents' stumblings, especially as you loved Mom in the middle of trauma. How we love to laugh with you as we learn how to "do family" and love all the fun people that God sends across our path. Life has never ever been dull with all of you. We love you over the top!

Contents

PART 1

The Nature of Trauma

Why Can't I Just Get Over It?

When Trauma Hits Home

Our Stories

We didn't plan to focus on the field of trauma. It just happened—slowly, painfully, and deeply. But we know beyond a shadow of a doubt that God has called us to bring Christ's healing to the traumatized. We've started a journey from staying aloof to engaging the world's pain. And we're not just counselors; we are fellow sufferers as well. We've experienced the deep wounds of trauma ourselves.

The stories in this chapter are different in many ways, but they share a common theme: we see the world differently because we've been touched by the reality of trauma. For me (Norman) my call involved a slow unfolding that was like the formation of a tapestry. On the other hand, for me (Julie) my own encounters with trauma formed the groundwork of the call to bring Christ's love to the traumatized, which crystallized in the overwhelming crucible of Ground Zero. And for me (Matt) the call to work with the traumatized came from my work as a pastor and my deep passion for the church to become an agent of healing in a broken world.

Norman's Story: Like a tapestry coming together

My journey into the field of trauma was like watching a number of threads come together to form a single tapestry. As a Christian counselor, I spent hours sitting and listening to the stories of broken lives, broken marriages, and broken souls. Over the years of listening to these stories, I always said to myself, "Yes, I hear your story, my friend, but there's something else in there. There's more to this story." Whether they could articulate it or not, underneath the brokenness of their lives, nearly every person who came to me for counseling had a story of trauma. And every trauma story contained the profound and soul-shattering wounds of loss and grief.

I knew these stories of a past trauma were still fueling their pain in the present. The trauma from the past haunted and controlled their lives. For example, a young woman came to see me whose life was shaken and traumatized years ago by a bone-jarring, building-toppling earthquake. Even many years later, when she finally came to see me for counseling, she still couldn't open a newspaper for fear that it might trigger some painful memories. As a seminary professor, I also met numerous young men who had come back from the Vietnam War, still shaken, still suffering from post-traumatic stress disorder. These stories of past trauma were legion. Everywhere I turned I seemed to hear stories about the lingering effects of past trauma and loss. Each story represented only a single thread, but the threads were definitely weaving a larger picture.

Of course I was sensitive to these stories because they intersected with my own story. My wife, Joyce, and I will never forget the words that were spoken by our doctor: "In the next hour your son's heart and lungs will fail." Shortly after that, our twenty-two-year-old son, Matthew, died. He was a profoundly retarded child, and at his death he was about eighteen months old mentally. He lived in our home until he was eleven and then lived at Salem

Christian Home in Ontario, California. At the age of twenty-one, Matthew developed a condition known as reflux esophagitis, a burning of the lining of the esophagus. He was given medications, but when that didn't work, Matthew went into the hospital for corrective surgery. Following the surgery, complications and infections set in. After a week had passed, additional surgery was performed, but Matthew never made it out of the hospital.

In the words of my wife, "Losing Matthew was a tremendous blow . . . but like any major loss, it also caused a number of additional or secondary losses. The routine we had followed was gone forever. We wouldn't have the special weekends in which he could come home and stay overnight, nor would we be able to stop by Salem to take him out to eat. . . . We faced future losses as well. Matthew would no longer be home on Thanksgiving or Christmas. . . . We couldn't call Salem anymore to see how he was doing, a topic of our conversation was gone, and certain phrases or expressions we would say to him would no longer be expressed."

Even now, several years after the death of our son, Joyce and I still experience stabs of grief on what would have been Matthew's birthday. And when March 15 rolls around each year, we're especially sensitive, because that's the day he died.

After we shared Matthew's story in the book *I'll Love You Forever*, individuals, couples, and families came to me and shared their stories of loss, grief, and trauma. Last year alone I worked with nine couples who had lost a child. They needed someone who could help them process the losses. They always started the conversation with these words: "We think you can understand our pain and loss. That's why we came to you."

People who have experienced trauma and loss know firsthand one of the sad truths about life: most people don't know how to deal with it. It's a strange and even terrifying topic for discussion. So we pretend that it doesn't exist or that it will go away. But trauma and its effects never just go away.

So I found my story of loss intersecting with the stories of many who had experienced trauma and loss. As I walked beside my fellow sufferers, they hungered to process the pain—if only someone would listen. I began to see the world through the eyes of the hurting and traumatized. For instance, I started to hurt for the four out of ten service men and women serving in Iraq who returned home still suffering from the effects of post-traumatic stress disorder. As I counseled the survivors of 9/11, I also realized that this event had traumatized so many people in this country who lost loved ones or even just watched the coverage on television. I especially thought of the children whose innocence was shattered by the vivid scenes from that horrible day.

Because the theme of trauma has cut so deeply into my life, I often find myself viewing the world through a unique lens—the lens of trauma. A few years ago I was watching a television show that was interrupted by a live news report about an enraged man on a Los Angeles freeway. As the news cameras rolled, thousands of people watched in horror as this man waved a Molotov cocktail in the air and threatened to kill himself on live television. Like everyone watching that day, I prayed and hoped for a peaceful solution. But I also said out loud (as if the news reporters could hear me), "Cut the tape! This man is going to blow himself to bits, and thousands of people, including hundreds of children, will have a scene of graphic violence etched on their minds for years to come. Please have some sense and turn off the cameras."

My experience with traumatized people trained me to look at this event through a different lens, leading me to ask different questions:

- What are the long-term effects of watching this violence?
- What kind of trauma will enter into the minds of this man's family members and close friends?
- How long will this violent image stay in people's minds?

- How will this intersect with the viewers' unresolved pain?
- How many children will be traumatized by this incident?

A trip to hurricane-ravaged New Orleans served to reinforce and deepen this commitment to view the world through the lens of trauma. On October 17, 2005, I landed in Baton Rouge to help with the Victim Chaplain Ministry. I wasn't prepared for what I encountered. What you and I saw in the media could never capture the reality of this event. There are no words to describe the devastation I saw in New Orleans. It was one thing to hear that eighty percent of the city was under water, but it was another to drive mile after mile, the only vehicle on side streets, and see nothing but crushed, shattered, and empty homes. From the poorest tiny structure to the expensive mansion, no house could withstand the force of hurricane Katrina. Whatever wasn't flattened was torn and twisted. I saw large boats hundreds of yards inland, heavy pianos hanging out of windows, and cars standing on end or perched on top of walls.

For most residents in the Ninth Ward (or the ghetto, as it is often described), there was nothing to return to in this district. The homes there and even miles away would need to be bulldozed. Wood furnishings as well as the soil were contaminated. There was nothing to restore or rebuild. It would take at least five years or longer to reconstruct. And where did one begin? It was overwhelming.

It's difficult to fathom the extent of the losses for hundreds of thousands of people in this area. They didn't just lose homes. They lost their history, possessions, and memories, family items to pass on to the next generation, neighbors, friends, a safe haven and familiar surroundings, church, pastor, security—the list goes on. According to the U.S. Department of Education, 372,000 children from kindergarten through high school were displaced by Katrina.

And it is estimated that 30 percent or 112,000 are likely to develop post-traumatic stress disorder.

One elderly woman, very upset and anxious over her losses, was invited to rest in our motor home while a worker went to where her home used to be and searched through the pile. The only personal item he could find was a picture frame, which she clutched in her arms. She was still holding on to it when she left, for it was the only possession that remained after sixty to seventy years of living there.

The deepest trauma involved the loss of loved ones. I listened to a conversation in which a middle-aged man called wanting to find his nine-year-old daughter whom he knew was dead. He was holding her hand as he climbed into the attic, but she slipped from his grasp and he never saw her again. She was afflicted with cerebral palsy and partially disabled. To speed up the identification process, he shared that she had a hip transplant with a titanium part. And if a family member's body was found, the funeral rituals of their culture had been lost, for friends and other family members had been relocated. There would be no marching with musicians, no pastor or church or support for their grief.

Of course, trauma isn't just about the Gulf War, 9/11, a deranged man on the freeway, or horrific hurricanes. Over the past twenty years I've learned that trauma, with its accompanying grief and loss, will cut into everyone's heart. So every time I want to ask someone, "How are you doing?" I add an extra emphasis to the question: "How are you *really* doing?"

Julie's Story: Like beginning a great adventure

About four years ago God beckoned me to a great adventure of faith. At the same time my husband also sensed that God was calling us to something beyond our wildest dreams. This adventure started quietly as my husband, a pastor in Minnesota, read an ad in a magazine for a church on Long Island that seemed like a perfect fit. We had prayed for this church profile ever since the day we met: a Christ-centered church in a multicultural, university setting. We applied for the job with low expectations because the church also had another 399 applicants. Through some miraculous circumstances, Matt was offered the job as senior pastor of the Three Village Church on Long Island, situated about fifty miles east of Manhattan.

So in June of 2001 we packed up our four children—then ages sixteen, fourteen, twelve, and ten—and left our warm home in Minnesota. Our children had many good friends in Minnesota and weren't thrilled about this crazy adventure. To be honest, their parents weren't exactly thrilled either! But we felt like God was calling us to a wild adventure, and we wanted to obey, although it meant leaving our beautiful home in Minnesota that we had built. We even had to leave our dog Sweetie behind.

Things were going quite well as we moved into the church parsonage, a seven-bedroom, 140-year-old Victorian house the size of the *Titanic*. We were adjusting to the unique New York accent, the frantic driving, boogey boards, sushi, New York delis, and loud conversations . . .

And then September 11 hit.

My fourteen-year-old son had just been in Tower 2 the Sunday before, and we were planning a family trip to New York City. While our children were in school, they heard a school official's frantic announcement: "If you get home and your parents aren't there, call 911 immediately." Later that evening, as we drove by the train station, we anxiously observed that the parking lot was full. My stomach turned as I pondered that some of those people would never return to their cars.

That night at dinner we struggled to help our children make some sense out of something we ourselves couldn't understand. Our youngest son put his hands over his ears and said, "I wish

15

no one had ever told me about this. These things aren't supposed to happen, especially to eleven-year-olds." I echoed his thoughts. For the next two months the only way my children could sleep was to put up a small tent in their room, often cuddling together with Matt, me, and our new dog, Dwight.

Eight days after September 11, I had the opportunity to travel with a group of people from McDonald's restaurant to serve food at Ground Zero. We had a trailer set up about a block from the site. All day long I stood and handed out hamburgers and Cokes to rescue workers, firemen, policemen and their dogs, and grieving civilians who were waiting to hear word of their loved ones. I was handed a huge stack of colorful stickers made by elementary students for firemen that said things like "You are my hero," "We love you," "Please pull out some live people." When I placed those stickers on the men, they often got tears, and sometimes I was able to pray with them.

We would often leave the trailer and drive to the street near Ground Zero (a large fence kept us from the hole where they were digging). On one occasion, I approached a man who looked very lost. I asked him if he could remember the last time he ate. He looked at me blankly and said, "I can't remember." I handed him a cheeseburger and a Coke and asked him what he was doing there. Handing me a picture with tearstains on it, he said, "This is my daughter, Danielle. She's only twenty-three, the only family I have—my wife died years ago. She was working in Tower 2, and I haven't heard from her since the morning of September 11." We both cried as I said I would pray for Danielle. He asked me to please just pray that they would find her alive today.

I spoke with one young fireman who looked grief-stricken and lost. He told me that he just wanted to pull out his buddies alive. He said, "I have at least six close friends in there."

I approached one volunteer, a huge man who had just removed his gloves, and gently asked him, "What happened to your hands?"

He said, "I'm a volunteer who works my regular job all day and comes here to dig all night. I have many friends that we can't find. For the first few days I dug with my bare hands because I was just frantic to find them. When you love your buddies as much as I do, you don't care if your hands hurt and bleed, you just want to find them."

About 9:00 p.m. I was asked to go to the bottom of the towers with a group of men in a golf cart to hand out food and drinks to workers who hadn't eaten for half a day. So we loaded up our little cart and hung on as we careened toward Ground Zero. As we got closer to the guts of the sight, my mind just couldn't comprehend it all. The television pictures don't convey what I saw that night. This scar in the ground was unfathomable! Sharp objects were sticking out of buildings, cars were burnt black, debris was protruding out of the ground, and the stench of the inferno was unbearable.

I recall feeling overwhelmed and confused; my brain couldn't process this. As I will share with you later in this book, I know about trauma firsthand. Sexual abuse, grief, a traumatic accident, cancer, post-abortion trauma, physical violence, depression—these traumas have cut into my soul. But the scene from Ground Zero left me speechless and disoriented. It was just too much.

And then I watched as a large circle of rescue workers surrounded a digging site, watching, listening, waiting for a tap, a breath, a cry, a sign of life. But there was nothing—only the sound of the big machines digging and the buckets being passed back and forth as the workers continued to dig and fill them.

I felt embarrassed as I looked at the pile. I had brought my camera but knew that I couldn't take any pictures. This was too personal, too painful to capture. They had their buddies in there, people they dearly loved. As I got off the cart and handed out cheeseburgers, I felt so surrounded by love. I saw love in action as I watched these men sacrifice their lives to save their buddies and others who were devastated. "We want to save just one," they kept saying.

As I dished out the hamburgers, I suddenly brushed against a sharp object that cut my leg. A group of six dust-covered rescue workers quickly surrounded me with concern. My leg was bleeding through my pants, and one guy tore off part of his shirt and tied it around my cut. I remember thinking about how quickly they responded to my wounds, and it dawned on me that they were probably excited to help someone who was alive. It was a very moving experience.

Later, as I walked toward a section of Tower 2, I tripped over a backpack, stepped on a discarded shoe, and then saw a piece of the building start to sway. As I froze with fear, a fireman pulled me out of the way and put his arm around me. Seeing my fear, he protected me until I could find the cart. Everyone kept saying, "Thank you; thank you for coming; thank you for feeding us in this place." Overcome with grief, I couldn't speak, but I wanted to say, "I deserve no thanks. You deserve thanks. You have taught me about love, about sacrifice, about Christlike compassion for those who hurt."

Something deep within me changed as I watched them dig, their tired bodies hunched over this massive pile of broken buildings. I had a deep desire to give like them: passionately and selflessly. As I was deep in thought, I looked up and saw a broken building with the windows blown out, a curtain waving through the window, and then above it a sliver of a moon. Next to the moon I watched the American flag waving in the breeze at the top of the building.

Scrawled on another building were the words "God is still here" and "God will heal our land." As we drove away on our little golf cart now empty of hamburgers and Cokes, I felt so very blessed to have this heart-wrenching experience. For some reason my safety didn't seem as important as it did before; I was being called by

God to get involved in the world's struggles and traumas. I decided that I didn't want to sit on the sidelines with my remote control anymore; I wanted to be in the middle of the battle. I went back to the McDonald's trailer and was sick to my stomach. It was so disturbing.

I couldn't afford to be aloof any longer. As I left Ground Zero that night and hopped on a train to go home, I offered God this prayer from the depths of my heart: *Lord Jesus, I am just one weak, ordinary woman, but PLEASE teach me how to love these people who have been so wounded by this atrocity. Please, Lord, show me how they feel; help me to experience some of what they have experienced.* With that prayer, God put me on a journey for the next three and a half years that rocked my life. This book represents the fruit from those years.

Matt's Story: Becoming agents of healing in a broken world

My journey into the field of trauma has been simple and direct: nearly every day I'm confronted with it. As the senior pastor of a church on Long Island, I work with competent, smart, and successful people. They are articulate and busy high-achievers. But underneath the surface, many individuals and families silently struggle with the lingering damage from traumatic life experiences. And, sadly, many more people just avoid the church because their past trauma isolates them from the "good church people" who seem so self-sufficient.

Both groups—the churchgoers and the church-avoiders—live in fear of the "potential trauma" that hangs in the air like secondhand smoke. For instance, as I write this, *Newsday*, Long Island's main newspaper, reported four stories of "ordinary" and "everyday" trauma. First, two boys pleaded guilty to an attempted Columbine-style shooting at one of our local high schools. Second, an intruder crept into the home of three grown sisters, attacking each of them and then fleeing into the night. Third, a young man who tried to break up a fight on a late-night train ride was assaulted as soon as he stepped off the train. Fourth, during the afternoon rush hour in Minneapolis, an eight-lane bridge connecting the Twin Cities collapsed with a deafening roar. Nearly fifty cars plummeted sixty-four feet into the Mississippi River below.

As I read the newspaper in a local restaurant, the waitress commented, "This is such a crazy world. I moved out of New York City to feel safe, but I don't feel safe here anymore either. There are too many crazy things happening all around us—and these crazy things could happen to any of us." Stories like this often tap into past traumas and create terror for future ones.

Tragically, most people try to cope with the past pain and the future fear isolated from God and one another. So as a pastor, my passion is to watch the living God create a safe community, a community where all people can encounter the healing balm of Christ. Recently I read the following quote from a leading expert on trauma: "Trauma and our responses to it cannot be understood outside the context of human relationships. . . . The most traumatic aspects of all disasters involve the shattering of human connections. . . . Because humans are inescapably social beings, the worst catastrophes that can befall us involve relational loss. As a result, recovery from trauma and neglect is also about relationships—rebuilding trust, regaining confidence, returning to a sense of security and reconnecting to love." [1]

When I read this vision for community and healing, my heart started pumping faster. That's exactly what the gospel offers to the entire human race: relationships of trust and security and love. Our new life begins with a relationship of love offered through the life, death, and resurrection of Jesus Christ. As we trust in him, we're ushered into a loving relationship with our heavenly Father. But this new life continues in community with others who have trusted Christ. This new community offers something beautiful and powerful to people living in the grip of past or potential trauma: healing and wholeness in Christ, hope in our suffering, and security forever in our relationship with God and with one another.

As more and more people in our fractured world encounter the pain of trauma, the church will have a more vital role to play in society. It's my hope and dream that the followers of Jesus will be the primary agents of healing in our broken world, holding forth the Word of Life in the midst of our world's chaos.

Our Hope for This Book

The scope of this book is much bigger than the bywords now etched in the minds of all Americans: *9/11* and *Ground Zero*. Based on our extensive counseling practice, we know that many more people have a smaller but no less traumatic "personal ground zero." These personal ground zero experiences may take the form of childhood sexual abuse, post-abortion trauma, rape, an eating disorder, physical abuse, your parents' divorce, the sudden loss of a loved one, or a tragic accident. Although these smaller stories may not appear in the national newspapers, for those who live these stories, the trauma slashes deep into the heart, leaving behind profound and permanent wounds.

We have crafted this book to offer a glimpse of our journey into the eye of trauma's storm. We share our heart for the traumatized. The stories and principles for dealing with trauma also derive from our extensive practice of counseling those who have been traumatized. But none of this is mere theory. Through circumstances beyond our control, we know the fear, confusion, and pain of trauma. We are fellow strugglers, not just experts. But more importantly, we want to tell a story of God's amazing grace to bring strength out of weaknesses, glory out of shame, and joy out of affliction. We know that trauma hurts, but we also know that we're on a healing path with Christ. We want to offer a tool that you can use on your own journey of healing from trauma. Please read it with an open heart, looking to Jesus as the author and perfecter of your faith (Heb. 12:2).

2

What Is Trauma?

(MATT AND JULIE WOODLEY
WITH NORMAN WRIGHT)

Bill's and Susan's Story. After a long week at work, Shawn relished the upcoming weekend with his wife, Susan, and their two-year-old son, Joey. Because Susan felt sick from her three-month pregnancy, Shawn and Susan's brother, Bill, volunteered to drive a few miles and pick up a pizza. As Shawn and Bill cruised through a green light, another motorist sped through his light, slamming into the driver's side of Shawn's compact car. A short, joyful ride for a pizza suddenly became a storm of trauma.

An hour after the accident Bill woke up on a hospital bed, bruised and battered but alive and whole. His first question was, "Where's Shawn? Is he okay?" A nurse calmly told him, "He's pretty banged up, but he's going to make it." An hour later, Bill's brother came into the room with tears in his eyes. "Where's Shawn?" Bill moaned. "What's wrong? Tell me he's going to make it." Bill's brother whispered slowly, "No, Bill, Shawn didn't make it. He died five minutes ago."

The trauma from a short drive for pizza would haunt this family for years. Susan was left with a two-year-old son. In six months she would give birth to a son who would never meet his father. Bill, who was driving the car at the time of the accident, would be haunted by grief and guilt. Every time he looked into his sister's face, he felt the full weight of that guilt.

Diane's Story. On an early March morning in 2007, an intruder crept into a home in the middle of Long Island where three grown sisters lay sound asleep. The assailant went from room to room, attacking each of them. The youngest of the women heard the screams from her sisters and fought off the man with her teeth and hands, biting his fingers and eventually pulling away his weapon. But before the man fled into the night, he had murdered one of the sisters and left another sister blind in one eye. The brutal intruder is still at large.

Still traumatized, the surviving sisters and their father (who had already survived the death of his wife in 1995) sold their family home and moved to an undisclosed location. "I had one fear," reported one of the sisters, "and it came true, that I would lose one of my sisters. I live forever with a broken heart." The other surviving sister said, "If I'm around a bunch of people I know, I get frightened. I wish I had a normal life, and I never will."[1]

Tom's Story. When he was in seventh grade, Tom enjoyed school, but at times he didn't know where he fit with his peers. Although he had two older brothers, his family never played together. His father often worked long hours seven days a week. Tom had never found his niche.

Until, that is, an English teacher discovered and affirmed Tom's gift of writing. When Mr. Jennings began to spend time with Tom, the boy felt flattered. Mr. Jennings even started to take Tom out for dinner and give him gifts. Soon the flattery and gifts turned into sexual abuse. The toll the relationship took on Tom was devastating. To the present day, Tom doesn't feel like he deserves to be a man. He has become heavily involved in the gay lifestyle, often numbing the pain with alcohol and cocaine. Tom describes himself with words like "defective" and "unmanly."

His shame from those events casts a cloud over his present life. The sexual abuse took place eight years ago, but the trauma from the abuse still haunts Tom.

My Story (Julie). This past August, after three years of living in our church's parsonage, we moved into a beautiful new home on a quiet street. Right after supper on a lovely evening, my husband took our youngest son to his soccer practice and I left for a short bike ride. As I rode toward West Meadow Beach on Long Island for the first time after being diagnosed with cancer two years earlier, I felt a surge of energy coursing through my body. I easily made the one-mile trek to the beach and then started back home. About one hundred feet from our house, my bicycle chain fell off and jammed into my pedal, stopping the bike and flinging me headfirst over the handlebars and onto the street. Although I have no memory of the accident, the emergency workers determined that I probably landed squarely on my head and right elbow and then skidded on my knees and forearms.

Fifteen minutes later my new neighbor found me lying on the street, tangled in my bicycle and soaked in blood. He wrapped me in a blanket and called for help. Matt and our youngest son arrived as the sun was setting and as the rescue workers loaded me into the ambulance—the most terrifying moment of their lives. I suffered a hematoma, another hemorrhage to the brain, a broken elbow, a cracked cheek bone, and a number of cuts and abrasions.

Months later I still struggled with dizziness and fatigue. I had no idea that a head injury would take so long to heal. For the next six weeks, I distinctly remember learning basic skills such as walking more than twenty-five feet and putting thoughts together in a coherent way. However, miraculously, I still don't remember any details about the accident. I only recall waking up in the lap of God.

But my son Wesley does remember the details of my accident. Wesley appeared on the scene just as they were loading me, strapped on a stretcher and nearly unconscious, into the waiting ambulance. Wes and my husband snuck through the police line and walked toward our home. As soon as Wesley saw my blue shoes sprawled on the pavement, he knew that the body on the stretcher was his mom. He was overcome with fear. For the next six months he couldn't verbalize how he felt—until we were almost in a car accident. Suddenly he started sobbing, and he blurted out, "You don't understand, Mom! That day was so hard because I saw your shoes and I thought you were dead." His pent-up emotions gushed out.

What Is Trauma?

Trauma is the response to any event that shatters your world. As you can see from these stories, trauma comes in different shapes and sizes, encompassing a vast array of human experiences. It's more than a state of crisis. Trauma leaves you feeling unsafe because your place of refuge has been invaded.

The word *trauma* comes from a Greek word that means "wound." It's a condition characterized by the phrase "I just can't seem to get over it." This experience is not limited to those who have gone through a war. We've seen it in the father who saw his daughter fatally crushed in an accident, women who were sexually abused as children, the survivors of a tragic car accident, or those whose homes have been invaded by burglars. We've seen it in the paramedic, the chaplain, and the nurse, and also in the survivor of a robbery, traffic accident, or rape. Trauma touches those subjected to pressure or harassment in the workplace. We've also seen it in the faces of those impacted by terrorist attacks or mass shootings on a college campus.

If you've ever been to a rodeo, you've probably seen a rider pursuing a steer. He guides his horse next to that galloping steer and at the precise moment leaps from his horse, grabs the steer's horns, and pulls it to a dusty halt. With the right amount of pressure at the right time, he literally throws that steer to the ground. When you experience trauma, you are thrown about like that steer. Your world turns wild, out of control, crazy. For some victims the trauma will last for years. For others it will last for as long as they live.

The wound of trauma can create a condition called PTSD, or post-traumatic stress disorder. It is not just an emotional response to troubling events; it's the expression of a persistent deregulation of body and brain chemistry. And brain chemistry can be altered for decades. Trauma creates chaos in our brain and causes an emotional as well as a cognitive concussion. Entering the world of trauma is like looking into a fractured looking glass. The familiar appears disjointed and disturbing; a strange new world unfolds.

Common Themes in Every Trauma Story

Trauma encompasses a vast range of human experiences, yet every story of trauma contains common themes. We have identified fourteen themes that occur in nearly every story behind an unhealed traumatic event.

1. Trauma can strike anyone.

Are some of us more susceptible to being traumatized than others? If I am emotionally healthy, if I came from a "healthy home," if I'm a strong Christian, will I be immune to this disorder? No. We're all susceptible to trauma; we're all at risk. Your previous mental stability, race, gender, level of education, emotional disorders, or lack of emotional disorders seem to make no difference, although your ability to handle life's ordinary stresses and your unique coping skills can help. But trauma can overwhelm any of us.

What does make a difference, more than anything else, is the intensity and degree of stress. Studies have identified fifty-eight general vulnerability factors as contributing to a person becoming traumatized. But researchers are still puzzled about which responses assist a person in adapting best to a traumatic event.[2]

If you end up traumatized, it's *not* because of a defect in you. Your reactions are normal in response to an abnormal event. Your personality doesn't alter the outcome of experiencing trauma, but trauma *does* impact your personality. Yes, we do vary in our responses and our capacity for endurance. Some people have better coping skills than others. Those who have a strong faith in Jesus Christ and an accurate understanding of life through the Scriptures have more resources to help them cope. But for all of us there comes a point in time when our defenses are overrun.[3]

There is one last factor to consider. Those who are involved in natural catastrophes seem to experience shorter and less intense PTSD than those involved in man-made disasters. If a natural disaster can be seen as an act of nature or God—*That's just life*—the survivors don't lose as much trust in others as do those involved in man-made disaster. That's why Oklahoma City, Columbine, New York City, and Virginia Tech have impacted us so much.

2. Trauma is often unpredictable.

On April 16, 2007, an ordinary day on the beautiful Virginia Tech campus, a college student shot and killed thirty-two classmates and professors and left more than twenty wounded. It was the worst mass shooting in modern American history. No one saw it coming. Although the killer was clearly a troubled young man, no one could have predicted that he would chain the door to Norris Hall, storm several classrooms, and unload more than 170 rounds of bullets before putting a bullet in his own head amid his victims. The events of April 16 were totally unpredictable.

Of course the unpredictability of trauma occurs in more ordinary events as well. For instance, on a Monday morning Kimberly showed up at work for a typical day as a bank teller. She was relaxed from a few days off and looked forward to an evening with her friends. Four years earlier, when Kimberly completed her job training, her bank managers trained her in the proper procedures for handling an attempted robbery. But in its entire history, this bank had never encountered an attempted robbery—until this ordinary Monday morning. A man approached Kimberly and slipped her a small bag and a hand-scrawled note that read "I have a gun. Fill this bag with money." Instantly, Kimberly froze in terror, forgetting everything she learned four years earlier in training. She managed to give him the money, dropping the money bag in the process. As the robber turned to leave, the next man in line whispered, "Did that man just rob you?" Kimberly was paralyzed by the complete unpredictability of this traumatic event.

The storms of trauma are like that. They often appear out of nowhere, usually when it's most inconvenient. After the shootings at Virginia Tech that left thirty-three dead and twenty-four injured, a history professor commented, "I feel assaulted, like someone came into my house and trashed it. . . . This was like a tornado coming down out of the sky, unpredictable and random." Like the unpredictability of a tornado, trauma strikes suddenly and leaves and uproots our lives and our security.

3. Trauma leaves us feeling unsafe.

What we used to see as a safe world is no longer safe. What we used to see as a predictable world is no longer predictable. Most people overestimate the likelihood that their lives are going to be relatively free from major crises or traumas, and they underestimate the possibility of negative events happening to them. Perhaps that's why we're so devastated and our core beliefs are shaken when they do. In my work with university students, I (Matt) noticed the "unsafe" feeling that students had after the Virginia Tech shootings. *If it can happen in Virginia,* our students asked, *why can't it happen right in our backyard at Stony Brook University?* After a major bridge collapsed in Minneapolis on August 1, 2007, hurling nearly fifty cars into the water below, almost every local news station started asking, "Are the bridges in New York safe? How will we ever be able to trust our bridges again?" After the attack on the three young women (mentioned earlier), one of their neighbors commented, "The neighborhood is really a quiet neighborhood ... [but] it is scary, you know, because you're afraid someone can break into your house."

If you've been feeling invulnerable and thinking, *It can't happen to me,* trauma will not only wound you and shake your beliefs, it will also fill your life with fear. Invulnerability is an illusion. You don't have to be a victim of trauma to suddenly feel extremely vulnerable. Just viewing photographs in the paper is sufficient to take you from the role of spectator to participant in the trauma. We all end up feeling, *If it can happen there, it can happen here.*

4. Trauma involves a loss.

At the heart of every trauma there is always some kind of a loss. Losses threaten our security, our sense of stability, and our well-being. Although a gradual loss is still painful, you can prepare for it to some degree. But a sudden, unexpected death may disrupt your ability to activate the emotional resources you need to cope with the loss. The more sudden, unexpected, and tragic the event, the greater the impact.

There are two types of loss associated with trauma—threatened loss and ambiguous loss. Threatened losses used to be reserved for the employees who read a memo describing a 30 percent personnel cut. Or the woman sitting in her doctor's office hearing these dreaded words: "There's a growth. I'll take a biopsy, and we'll let you know the results in a week." Or it could be the words of a spouse saying, "I'm thinking of divorcing you." Threatened losses make us feel powerless, like a victim waiting for the bad news. There's nothing you can do. Threatened losses also leave us on edge, suspicious, somewhat subdued, sad and angry, waiting and wondering.

Trauma counselors have also identified another type of loss—ambiguous loss. Ambiguous loss occurs when we yearn for closure but it remains out of reach. For instance, loved ones want to see the remains of a body, but instead they have to live with ambiguity and uncertainty. With this ambiguous loss, they are left baffled, immobilized; they have difficulty problem solving; and they may never be able to achieve the detachment that is necessary for normal closure. There's an endless searching. The loss continues as the family alternates between hope and hopelessness. They deal with the death but want closure. The family is denied the rituals that support a real loss. Thus their grief is frozen.

5. Trauma makes us feel overwhelmed.

As I (Julie) sorted through the trauma in my life, I often felt like my mind was overloaded. When I was forty years old, I developed an eating disorder, losing sixty pounds in two months. I had allowed the "overwhelmingness" of earlier trauma to build up and bury me. Usually, I could pretend and keep the pain at bay, but this time the "face" came off and I fell apart, crying for hours at a time, forgetting how to do simple things like putting the laundry into the washing machine.

Some people feel overwhelmed right away; others (like me) sometimes hold their trauma inside until it comes out in tidal waves. Being overwhelmed with trauma can manifest itself in many forms. Some try to hide from their pain with addictions in an attempt to numb the feeling of being overwhelmed. I have seen eating disorders surface when people (especially young women) become overwhelmed with traumatic events. They don't know what to control when things feel so overwhelming, so they try to control their weight. All of these symptoms are ways to "manage" the pain and confusion of trauma.

6. Trauma is often unspeakable.

Trauma is indescribable. After the shooting deaths on the Virginia Tech campus, one student-survivor struggled for words: "It was just unbelievable. . . . It's indescribable." Elie Wiesel, a Nobel Peace Prize recipient and a survivor of Auschwitz, and his wife were in a taxi in Manhattan when the first Trade Tower was hit on September 11, 2001. They went home and watched on television. He said, "We watched the first pictures. They were both surreal and biblical: The flames, the vertical collapse and the disappearance of the world's two proudest towers. Many of us were stunned into silence. Rarely have I felt such a failure of language."[4]

Elie Wiesel says that language is inadequate for the task of describing trauma, and yet at the same time, he contends that "not to transmit an experience is to betray it."

7. Trauma can isolate us from others.

Catherine considered herself a good mother to her three small girls. But when Catherine's daughter Margie was just two years old, their life started to unravel. Her husband, a schizophrenic, stopped taking his meds, and the next years were marked by chaos, horror, and pain. He spiraled downward, threatening to kill Catherine if she didn't do exactly what he wanted. The girls suffered many beatings and watched in horror as he often beat their mother.

As Margie came to see me (Julie) for counseling, she still suffered the effects of this deep trauma. And even worse, she developed an eating disorder and isolated herself from others as she tried to detach herself from the pain he inflicted upon her. Trauma often has this effect on us. We feel shameful and abnormal, and we deal with these feelings by pulling away from others. We don't want anyone to see the "badness" or "brokenness" inside us. We feel like we just can't relate to "normal" people anymore because trauma has made us so "abnormal."

8. Different people may interpret trauma in different ways.

Some events would be threatening for anyone, whereas some would be threatening *just for you*. People respond differently to traumatic events. Your beliefs, ideas, expectations, and perceptions all work together as you determine whether or not a situation is a crisis.

Two people can view the same event differently, depending on several factors. For instance, you appraise the death of a close friend from several viewpoints: How close the relationship was, how often you were in touch with that friend, how you have responded to other losses, and how many losses you have experienced recently. A woman deeply involved in her husband's life perceives his death differently than does a close friend, a business associate, or the uncle who saw the deceased once every five years.

9. Trauma can change or challenge our view of God.

In his book *How Can It Be All Right When Everything Is All Wrong?* Lewis Smedes describes the trauma of losing a child:

> The other night, trying to sleep, I amused myself by trying to recall the happiest moments of my life. I let my mind skip and dance where it was led. I thought of leaping down from a rafter in a barn, down into a deep loft of sweet, newly mown hay. That was a

superbly happy moment. But somehow my mind was also seduced to a scene some years ago that, as I recall it, must have been the most painful of my life. Our firstborn child was torn from our hands by what felt to me like a capricious deity I did not want to call God. I felt ripped off by a cosmic con-artist. And for a little while, I thought I might not easily ever smile again.[5]

In the aftermath of trauma, grief, and loss, Smedes's view of God changed from a loving heavenly Father to a "capricious deity I did not want to call God." His heart shifted from trust to feeling "ripped off by a cosmic con-artist." Trauma often shatters our faith. Of course, on the other side of a shattered faith, many followers of Jesus claim that the trauma actually helped deepen and refine their faith, clarifying their vision of God's love and holiness. But the refining process is always painful, and there are no shortcuts around this spiritual shattering and rebuilding.

10. Trauma produces "hyper-arousal," "hyper-alertness," and "hyper-sensitivity."

Trauma expert Judith Herman calls *hyper-arousal* the "cardinal symptom of post-traumatic stress disorder." "After a traumatic experience, the human system of self-preservation seems to go onto permanent alert, as if the danger might return at any moment . . . the traumatized person startles easily, reacts irritably to small provocations and sleeps poorly."[6]

Trauma literally changes the way our brains process information. In effect, trauma overrides our brains' "alarm system" that controls our behavior. When we've been traumatized, our behavior becomes hypersensitive. It overreacts to normal stimuli.

For instance, as a child victim of physical abuse, I (Julie) was hit or slammed in the head on a number of occasions. Now whenever anyone attempts to pat me or accidentally bumps me on the head, I panic. In fact, this past week while attending my son's basketball game, a stray ball came flying toward my head and for a split second

I thought I was under attack. My system of self-preservation kicked into alert, and I was startled and reacted with intensity.

The strong emotions trauma survivors experience—fear, anxiety, anger—affect your body, particularly your adrenaline output. When people say they are pumped up, it's usually because of an adrenaline rush that puts the body into a state of hyper-alertness. Adrenaline increases blood pressure, heart rate, muscle tension, blood-sugar level, and pupil dilation.

There's a name for this condition; it's called the "fight or flight" reaction. The fight occurs because of the increase of adrenaline. But if the adrenaline pumps in even more, you end up in the freeze response. You end up moving and thinking in slow motion. Everything seems to have shut down. This condition is often evidenced by symptoms such as difficulty sleeping, periods of irritability for unknown reasons, difficulty concentrating, and anxiety over crowds and being easily startled.[7]

During a traumatic event, when the heart begins to race, breathing is difficult and muscles tighten. Some, in their attempt to make sense of what is happening to them, mislabel their bodily responses as catastrophic: "I'm going crazy," "I'm going to collapse," "I'm going to have a heart attack," "I'm dying." Some never correct their labeling of these bodily responses. So anytime their heart pounds or they have difficulty breathing, they misinterpret what is happening and end up with a panic attack.[8] The surge of emotions—like fear—can be so overwhelming that a person feels as though a dam has collapsed and the raging waters are totally out of control.

We work with many people who are paralyzed by fear. Sometimes they fear making a decision, gaining another's disapproval, or taking a stand. They may fear that other people don't like them. And even worse, they fear breaking out of this pattern they are trapped in. Others are paralyzed in some other way by their trauma. Physical paralysis is a terrible thing—to be locked up, immobilized, so that your body can't function and respond to the messages of your mind, is frustrating. But it is even more frustrating when the paralysis is the limitation or immobilization of the mind.

11. Traumatized people often reexperience the trauma.

Thoughts, pictures, dreams, nightmares, or even flashbacks of what occurred may take up residence in your life. Sometimes they slip into your mind like a video stuck on continuous replay. This sensitivity can become so extreme that an event can trigger a flashback and make you feel and act as if you were experiencing the original trauma all over again.

Trauma expert Judith Herman calls this *intrusion*. "Long after the danger is past," she observes, "traumatized people relive the event as though it were continually recurring in the present. They cannot resume the normal course of their lives, for the trauma repeatedly interrupts. It is as if time stops at the moment of the trauma. The traumatic moments become encoded in an abnormal form of memory, which breaks spontaneously into consciousness, both as flashbacks during waking states and as traumatic nightmares during sleep."[9]

A friend of mine (Norman) who is a Vietnam vet often experiences this at police funerals as he sees the flag-draped coffin. I've been with those who can't watch certain movies on TV because of the effect the movies have on them. I've been with a person who, when the loud rumbling of a truck went by, reacted as though a major earthquake was hitting again, similar to the one that had traumatized him.

A combat veteran walks down a street and hears a car backfire. He dives behind a tree to hide from the enemy and recalls the memories of his friends who were blown up in front of him. A victim of rape or sexual abuse has a flashback when making love to his or her spouse. An accident victim has a flashback at the sight of a car wreck or blood. Someone sees an object falling from a building and once again sees people jumping to their deaths from the World Trade Center.

Reminders, or *triggers*, may include the anniversary of the event. As the date draws near, the intensity of the actual trauma can build. Holidays and other family events can create strong emotional responses. It's possible for a traumatized person to be set off by something they see, hear, smell, or taste. In the case of abuse, a confrontation with the abuser may bring back emotional or physical reactions associated with the abuse.

12. Trauma leads to feelings of helplessness.

Physical trauma can affect a person in two ways. Obviously, some part of the body is impacted with such a powerful force that the body's natural protection, such as the skin or bones, can't prevent the injury, and the body's normal, natural healing capabilities can't mend the injury without some assistance.

Perhaps not as obvious, though, is the emotional wounding caused by trauma. Your psyche can be so assaulted that your beliefs about yourself, your spirit, your dignity, your sense of security, your will to grow, and life itself are damaged. You end up feeling helpless. In trauma you have difficulty bouncing back because you feel de-realization ("Is this really happening?") and depersonalized ("I don't know what I really stand for anymore"). Trauma leads to *feelings of hopelessness* because there was no way to stop what happened or the memories of what happened. So your level of optimism begins to crumble.

In his book entitled *Failure to Scream*, Robert Hicks writes: "When trauma hits our rationality becomes a curse. We are not like animals. . . . We are *Homo sapiens* (Latin for "thinking man"). We think about our tragedy, and our thinking can drive us crazy. The replay of the event, the flashback, even the smells, bring up reminders of the trauma. As rational beings we seek the rationale in the trauma. When none is found, the traumatic blow is heightened. The meaninglessness of the event can drive us to despair."[10]

13. Trauma doesn't make sense.

We all want a reason for what happens to us. We want to know "why" so that we can once again have a sense of order and predictability about life. But sometimes we must live our lives with unanswered questions. If you believe in a morality that says, "Right will always prevail and so will justice," what do you do when traumatic events that seem unfair creep into your life? What do you do when you expect the good guys to always win and the bad guys to always lose, and it doesn't turn out that way? You won't be the first or the last to cry out against injustice. Listen to Job: "If I cry out concerning wrong, I am not heard. If I cry aloud, there is no justice" (Job 19:7 NKJV). We want answers, we expect answers, we plead for answers, but sometimes Heaven remains silent. That's when our faith undergoes a crisis, in addition to whatever else is impacting us.

14. Trauma is not incurable; recovery is possible.

This chapter was written to alert you to the reality of trauma. It can happen to anyone at any time. And it cuts deep into the human heart. But remember that there is another side to trauma. The current research on those traumatized indicates that the majority of victims say they eventually benefited from the trauma in some way. How did they benefit? There was a change of values, a greater appreciation for life, a deepening of spiritual beliefs, a feeling of greater strength and appreciation, and a building of relationships. *You can promote healing through understanding.* The more you learn about trauma for yourself or for others, the more you will feel in control of your life.

In other words, you start to see yourself as a survivor and not a victim of traumatic events. We believe that the person who has a relationship with Jesus Christ and a biblical worldview has the greatest potential to become a survivor. Trauma can actually become a redemptive source of healing and blessing in your life and beyond your life. Look at what Scripture says about this:

> Blessed be the God and Father of our Lord Jesus Christ, the Father of mercies and God of all comfort; who comforts us in all our affliction so that we will be able to comfort those who are in any affliction with the comfort with which we ourselves are comforted by God. For just as the sufferings of Christ are ours in abundance, so also our comfort is abundant through Christ. But if we are afflicted, it is for your comfort and salvation; or if we are comforted, it is for your comfort, which is effective in the patient enduring of the same sufferings which we also suffer.
>
> 2 Corinthians 1:3–6 NASB

I've had people ask me (Norman), "How do I know I'm growing and getting better?" First of all, you have to develop a new way of looking at progress. It may be slow. There may be regressions. You need to focus on the improvements rather than on the times you feel stuck. One man told me that he rated his progress each month on a scale of one to ten, as well as his entire journey of healing at any one time. That helped him understand his own progress.

How can you tell if you're progressing and moving ahead? First, you can expect to see a reduction in the frequency of symptoms. Second, the intensity of fear you struggled with over the presence of these symptoms will diminish. One of the most disheartening fears is the fear of going crazy or insane. This fear will also diminish. Anger and grief, which exist hand in hand, will lessen. Third, what remains can be directed into positive directions. Candy Lightner, whose daughter was killed by a drunk driver, founded Mothers Against Drunk Driving (MADD). A friend of mine traumatized by the Vietnam War spends time each week using his energy to help the men in our local veterans hospital. He and his Alaskan husky take the men to worship service and other activities.

This doesn't happen in a day, a week, or even a year. Healing is slow, and it usually grinds its way through a series of fairly predictable stages. In the next chapter we'll analyze the common stages traveled by the traumatized.

3

The Emotions of Trauma

Anger

(NORMAN WRIGHT)

They hit with the intensity of a tornado and the suddenness of an earthquake. They won't go away when you want them to, and there's no way to evict them. They're like a runaway train whose brakes have burned out. You feel totally out of control. Even though you may question the necessity of their presence, they do have a purpose. What do we call these "unfriendly" companions? *Emotions. Feelings.*

During a trauma, you may experience many kinds of emotions, and perhaps some feelings you've never experienced before. It's not just the presence of the emotions that bothers you, it's their intensity. Some of them may feel unbearable, even toxic.

When you understand that feeling an emotion is an unavoidable human condition, and you know what to expect from emotions, you will handle them better. Many believe they are alone in their experience of such intense feelings: "No one else is like I am." This misbelief keeps them from accepting their feelings, learning from them, and moving on to recovery. When trauma happens, there is an overload of emotions. And too often they have no release; instead, they are filed away.

But what happens when intensely painful emotions brought on by trauma are stored intact in your nervous system for prolonged periods of time? These traumatic experiences will significantly color and shape your daily experiences until they are resolved. Merely talking or thinking about an emotionally painful experience will not always release the pain. Your *intellect* cannot resolve what is *emotionally* imprinted.

Remember that if you're a trauma survivor, your anger and grief are intimately related. You may have rage at what happened as well as grief over the loss. "The relative importance of grief versus anger is not really an issue—it simply varies from one trauma survivor to the next. You may be volcanic in your rage, but have yet to shed a single tear over your losses. Or you may have grieved profoundly, but have yet to confront your rage. Or you could be out of touch with both."[1] It's so much easier to be angry than sad. When you're angry you feel powerful and strong, but in grief you feel like a collapsed balloon, vulnerable, weak and hurting.[2]

Rage and anger are trauma's offspring. They often frighten the one experiencing the emotions as much as those on the receiving end. And they are often misdirected at those not responsible for what has occurred. But intense anger is common and for good reasons.

Anger won't draw others close to you but rather create a greater distance. It tends to be an isolating emotion. Family and friends may be bewildered at how to help you or how to respond to you. Their tendency will be to distance themselves from you, which

42

can feed your anger. The uncertainty of not knowing when an explosion is likely to occur is uncomfortable, and so the answer is isolation.

But the reality is that anger and even rage are common responses at a time of great loss. They are emotions that are as natural to all of us as are joy, fear, and sadness. Because a person is injured emotionally in trauma, anger is a normal response to being threatened. Its purpose is not to cripple us nor others but to help us survive. It is a secondary emotion usually caused by fear, hurt, or frustration. It serves as a protective crust that doesn't allow others to see our real pain and vulnerability.

For some who have been traumatized, the most accessible emotion at this time is anger. We use it to protect our hearts from experiencing pain and grief. This is why many will deny being angry, for to do so is to admit to the pain or grief or what created it.

There may be confusion about one's own anger. It is painful and pushes others away, and yet it is an appropriate response to some of the trauma some have experienced. Anger is full of energy that can be used for change and healing, or it can get out of hand and be damaging to oneself as well as others.[3]

Anger won't just fade away by itself. It sits, festers, and grows, searching for something to unload upon. And if it's not discharged, it burrows into your life in the form of anxiety and/or depression.

For those who experience trauma, anger is usually the least painful emotion to acknowledge. The focus of anger is outside of yourself, and you can admit to being angry without admitting the existence of other emotions such as fear, shame, or sadness. Anger helps distract us from these emotions by overriding them. Whereas the other emotions lead to a feeling of helplessness, anger leads us to a sense of control.

Anger has been described in the following ways:

43

You could be angry at yourself for being alive and well while someone else isn't. Or it could be at something you said or wished you had said for "not being yourself."

You could be angry because others "don't understand. They don't get it that you aren't going to get back to normal." And you're also angry because you're stuck in time while everyone else goes on living as if nothing had happened.

Hospital staffs, doctors, paramedics, friends, relatives, and funeral directors may be on the receiving end of your anger.[4]

Anger is a sign of protest. It's a natural and predictable emotion during a trauma or after a loss. It's a reaction against something that shouldn't have happened. It's a new way of fighting back when you feel helpless. Your perception of the way things are, or the way they should be, has been altered. Your belief system has been damaged. Anger is a normal reaction when you are deprived of something you value.

Expressions of anger against the injustices of life have always been with us. In the Bible, we find anger expressed in the Psalms and the books of the prophets. Job expressed anger at God, as did Jonah and Elijah.

Hundreds of years ago the American Indians shot arrows into the air to drive away evil spirits. We still do this, but we do it in a different way. We shake our fists, we verbalize, we write letters, and in some cases, we file lawsuits.

Society doesn't always know how to respond to our anger, and neither do many people in the church. That's because they often have an incorrect perspective of Scripture on this subject, and they attempt to project that perspective on others.

Let's take a look at some of the typical ways we direct our anger to avoid dealing with our pain.

Too often there is no appropriate object on which to vent our anger, so we begin looking for anything. Whom do we get angry at most often? God. We blame him—he shouldn't have done this, or he shouldn't have allowed that. He's supposed to do things right—the way we want it!

When we blame God, we can unnerve and unsettle other people. They may respond with Christian clichés or try to convince us that our anger at God is irrational. They fail to realize that nothing they say will help, because we are living on emotions at this point. Even though we may be raising questions, we're not really looking for answers.

People who recover successfully from trauma vent their anger rather than stuff it. They realize that to deny anger buries it alive, and someday there will be a resurrection. Buried anger can lead to addiction, alcohol abuse, and depression. It can blow up on others or burst inward with depression or other self-destructive behavior. But when anger is expressed to God, it can be analyzed and dealt with, and can lead to a rediscovery of the character and purposes of God.

You may be angry at the unfairness of the world—the unfairness of life itself. In 1995 in Los Angeles, a garbage truck pulled alongside a school bus loaded with children. A part of the apparatus malfunctioned and a large steel beam shot through the window of the bus, killing two young students instantly. Why them? Why so young? Why not the irresponsible ones? We raise these questions in vain. Because they are unanswerable, anger, disillusionment, and even irrationality become part of our emotional state.

After the crash of TWA Flight 800 into the waters off Long Island, New York, there was an outburst of anger on many fronts. That day a small town in Pennsylvania lost several high school students and chaperones on their way to France for two weeks of study. Even one death in a small community is felt by almost everyone, but when several are killed, the whole community plunges into crisis. The unfairness of losing so many from a small area generates an outburst against the unfairness of the whole world.

The loss of the men and women working in the World Trade Center and the rescue workers who perished trying to save them was a crushing experience. Our country was put into shock and grief.

Our anger may also be directed at other people. Family members of those killed on TWA Flight 800 were angry because victims were recovered slowly. And because details were announced from the media rather than by the proper authorities, they were angry at TWA, the media, the recovery workers, and the politicians.

There was smoldering anger in our nation against those who perpetrated the devastation in Oklahoma City in 1995 and New York City in 2001. There was visible anger at the terrorists and with the countries that harbored such people. We're angry at terrorists and nations who harbor terrorists, and we *should* be angry.

We even get angry at those who haven't had to experience what we've gone through. Because they haven't experienced, or we think they haven't experienced, the devastation that we have, part of us wants them to have to suffer what we've suffered. It's unfair—why should they be let off the hook?

Because we believe the tragedy or trauma shouldn't have happened, we look for something or someone to blame—a doctor, a hospital, an organization, a CEO, an accountant, a bus driver, or anyone we perceive as having somehow participated in the crisis. Sometimes our anger is vented toward anyone who is around, especially family members.

The bereaved get angry at the physician who tried in vain to help a loved one. Fire and flood victims get angry at the police and firefighters who were unable to save their homes. Widows often feel anger toward close family members after the first few weeks of bereavement. They feel overprotected and overcontrolled, or they feel unsupported and disappointed because they expected assistance from others.

46

We may get angry at those who fail to reach out and support us during our time of trouble. When we hurt, we want to be acknowledged. We don't want people to pretend that everything is okay. It isn't. In some cases it never will be the same. Of course, part of the reason we end up feeling isolated is because no one has taught us how to minister to each other during a time of need. Fortunately, this is starting to change.

Sometimes, if our loss was the death of a loved one, we may feel anger at the one who died. Survivors sometimes feel deserted or victimized. The loss of a spouse or a parent may leave us with the responsibility of what they left undone. Often anger comes because we feel out of control, powerless, and victimized.

We may direct our anger inward. Women are more likely to do this, while men generally turn anger outward. Anger turned inward is quite common after physical loss as well as when one is the victim of a crime. Intense self-directed anger can be immobilizing.

Anger can also wear an ugly face, as evidenced by its often destructive results. People seem to go to extremes in their demonstration of anger, either outwardly or inwardly. Turn it outward too much, and it destroys others. Turn it inward too much, and it destroys us.

The first time we see the effects of anger in Scripture, they are very destructive. "But on Cain and his offering he did not look with favor. So Cain was very angry, and his face was downcast. Then the LORD said to Cain, 'Why are you angry?'" (Gen. 4:5–6).

Cain was angry at his brother because Abel's sacrifice was acceptable and his own was not. Inwardly Cain experienced anger, and the result was murder (see Gen. 4:8). Cain was alienated from his brother, from other people, and from God. His anger led to murder and to extreme loneliness.

Not only did Cain misuse the emotion, but so did Esau, Saul, the Pharisees, Attila the Hun, Adolf Hitler, and rulers in most of the countries of the world. Our history is a tragic drama of hostility and domination.

Anger motivates a person to hate, wound, damage, annihilate, despise, scorn, loathe, vilify, curse, ruin, and demolish. Under anger's curse, a man will ridicule, retaliate, laugh at, humiliate, shame, criticize, bawl out, fight, crush, offend, or bully another person. All of these are definitely negative manifestations of anger.

Most everything in life has a price tag. Go into any store and rarely will you find anything that is free. Purchasing a new car may give us a feeling of elation, comfort, and prestige, but it costs. Expressing our anger can be a relief. It can influence or even control a situation. But it too has a price tag. Some of the costs may be obvious, such as a strained relationship—resistance or withdrawal of others when we come near them—or a tension-filled marital relationship with spouses who are now combatants rather than lovers. Even though there are personal physiological costs to anger, the greatest price to be paid is in our interpersonal relationships. Remember:

The power of anger after trauma is such that it feels like something destructive that will blow apart the mechanisms of coping and relationship. When properly appropriated, however, anger, instead of demanding and fueling revenge, is productive energy that creates a new understanding of the world. Anger, like grief, must run its course along pathways and time periods that are not of our choosing. Anger, however, cannot become healing or transformative if left on its own. It has to be respected and invited into consciousness before it will share its power. The real danger of anger is not the feeling itself, but the ways in which the attempt to contain it hollow out one's humanity rather than enhance it. Anger becomes destructive when it is used to diminish instead of serving as passion for change.[5]

How do you deal with anger in a positive way? You admit it, you accept it, and you release it in a healthy way. You use anger's energy to do something constructive. Mothers Against Drunk Driving (MADD) was founded because of the constructive use of anger directed toward a major problem in our society—drinking and driving. The MADD organization has made society aware of the problem of drunk drivers on our roads and highways and has helped to establish and reinforce laws to prosecute those who victimize others through their negligence.

There are many other examples of anger directed to constructive ends. A family who lost their son in a swimming accident at a lake organized a group of parents to convince resort managers and fish and game officials to post warning signs about water hazards to help prevent other similar tragedies.

A young mother whose two-year-old son died in the cancer ward of a hospital developed a cooperative program among fifteen churches in her city to set up support groups for parents of children who have died. In addition, each church solicited huge toy donations from merchants and families for the hospital pediatric ward.

Actress Theresa Saldano almost lost her life in a premeditated violent attack. She was stabbed again and again, and required more than a thousand stitches in her body. The attack left her with feelings of terror, intense pain, and rage. In her book *Beyond Survival*, she said it was her rage that gave her the energy to fight pain, death, and the sick desires of her assailant. It was also her rage at society's treatment of victims that gave her the vision to form a victim advocacy group called "Victims for Victims."

I don't know if anger over the accident that paralyzed him is what prompted Christopher Reeve to accomplish what he did. But he worked hard to gain financial support, increase public and government awareness, and lobby for new legislation to help victims of spinal cord damage. He wrote each United States senator personally, and helped to raise millions of dollars for research.[6]

Perhaps you could write a letter (don't mail it!) to whomever you're angry at and then sit in a room and read it aloud. During my counseling sessions in New York after the World Trade Center disaster, I had numerous people write an angry letter to the terrorists. Many found release by journaling each day to release pent-up feelings of anger. The point is, those who move ahead come to grips with their anger in constructive ways.

A friend of mine, Jessica Shaver, wrote the following poem that depicts what so many people have discovered.

I Told God I Was Angry

I told God I was angry.
I thought He'd be surprised.
I thought I'd kept hostility
quite cleverly disguised.

I told the Lord I hate Him.
I told Him that I hurt.
I told Him that He isn't fair,
He's treated me like dirt.

I told God I was angry
but *I'm* the one surprised.
"What I've known all along," He said,
"you've finally realized.

"At last you have admitted
what's really in your heart.
Dishonesty, not anger,
was keeping us apart.

"Even when you hate Me
I don't stop loving you.
Before you can receive that love,
you must confess what's true.

"In telling Me the anger
you genuinely feel,

it loses power over you,
permitting you to heal."

I told God I was sorry
and He's forgiven me.
The truth that I was angry
has finally set me free.

Many are afraid of experiencing their anger for fear that it may
spark a flaming torment that will rage out of control. Often this
occurs because of having to stifle their anger in the past, especially if they were abused. The longer anger has been inhibited,
the larger the pile.

The best way to handle anger and rage is in doses, small man-
ageable doses. It just doesn't work to deal with all of your anger
at once. One way of handling this is to divide your anger into two
categories—anger at yourself and then justified anger at whatever
or whoever created the traumatic experience. Some have found it
helpful to decide which is the dominant feeling: self-blame (which
often gets turned on others) or other blame. Start with the dominant one and each day set aside some time and write just two
sentences. For example:

I am angry at myself because . . .
I am angry at others because . . .

And then face this anger—discover its real source, identify whether
it's valid or not, decide whether you want it in your life anymore,
say goodbye to it, and tell it, "You're no longer needed."[7]

Do you have a safe place to vent your anger? Some have "anger
rooms" in their houses. It's healthy to create a safety zone for
yourself.

There are other ways to handle anger. Some have found help
by determining the cost factor of anger. It can give payoffs but
can also come with enormous costs.

The payoffs:

I care.

I feel in control.

It lets me feel something.

It gives me energy.

It's a sign that something needs fixing.

It protects me.

It clears the air.

Others respond and finally hear me.

The costs:

It hurts relationships.

It messes up my joy.

It teaches my kids to blow up.

I feel guilty.

It increases conflict.

People don't want to be around me.

It covers the real stuff.

It blocks communication.

My sex life suffers.

My body shows the wear and tear.[8]

Personalize your own list below so you can see the payoffs and costs of your anger.

The payoffs (good things) of my anger are:

_____

_____

_____

_____

_____

The costs (bad things) about my anger are:

_____

_____

_____

_____

_____

Someone has said that anger in the present is often an unhealed hurt button from the past that has been pushed. There will be times when the only way to get rid of your anger and feelings of revenge is to face the fact that you can't do anything to change what happened to you or to prevent a similar occurrence in the future. Then begin to give up a portion of your anger or resentment each day. One trauma victim said:

> I finally realized that holding on to my anger kept me victimized. As much as I wanted someone to pay, I knew it wouldn't happen. So I decided on a 90-day plan. I would allow myself to keep 10 percent of my anger since I know I'm human and won't be perfect. But each day for ninety days I would give up 1 percent of my anger. The fact that I had a goal and then developed a plan really encouraged my recovery. Each day I spent fifteen to twenty minutes identifying who or what I wanted to avenge. I wrote it out each time and then put it in the form of a brief letter. I stood in a room and read it out loud unedited. Sometimes it wasn't pretty. And sometimes I read it to a friend because it helped having a live body there.
>
> Each day I wrote the phrase, "I forgive you for . . ." and then put down the first reason I could think of for not forgiving. It was like I was full of rebuttals against forgiving. I would always end the morning by reading a praise psalm out loud. Then I would lift my hands to the Lord and give Him my anger for the day. Then I thanked Him for what He was doing, even if I didn't feel like it. I discovered many things through this: I was full of bitterness. It kept me pinned down and stuck. I didn't want to forgive. They didn't deserve it.

But I kept at it. I wondered after thirty days if I'd made even a 3 percent improvement. But by the time sixty days were over I felt ahead of schedule. I was improving; I was growing; I got well. Sometimes the anger and grief still hit me. I can live with that even if it's a companion the rest of my life. I have days and weeks when I feel whole again. Praise God for this.

Taking positive steps like this will help you make the shift from victim to survivor. *Believing* that you can become a survivor will accelerate this process.

Perhaps you've been fighting your feelings of anger and rage. Instead of letting them exist, you've tried to prevent them from breaking into your life. You've tried to deny them or turn them away. My question is, "Has it worked?" Probably not. The more you fight this presence, it seems the emotion you're battling has more control and gains a foothold in your life at this time. So if what you're doing isn't working, why keep doing it? There's a better way to respond. So let's try it.

Instead of resisting or trying to block the emotion when it occurs, welcome it. That's right, welcome it, whether it's anger, rage, fear, guilt, sadness, or something else. By doing this you take pressure off of yourself and lessen the power of the feeling. You could say,

Welcome, anger. I wondered where you've been. You haven't been here for a while, so welcome back. You've been here before, so I know I can handle you. I also know there's a reason or purpose for you being here so we'll try to determine what that is. And this time, it won't be just you and me interacting and responding. I've invited someone else to be present with us who can help you serve your purpose and begin to diminish. His name is Jesus and he, too, was traumatized at the cross. He came to bring redemption and forgiveness of sin and to bring healing to our pain. Jesus, the Son of God, will take over for me and face your purpose and what you want. So I will let him lead us as I give you to him.

54

The Emotions of Trauma

Guilt, Fear, and Depression

(NORMAN WRIGHT)

The emotions of trauma are many and varied. We're going to touch on just a few more that are most common.

Guilt

Our first is a frequent companion of trauma: guilt. Often accompanied by shame, guilt works its way into the grief process. This is normal and can often be traced to our tendency to place blame, but now we end up pointing the finger back at ourselves.

Guilt is present in any trauma when we feel that we've fallen short in some way or have violated something we believe in. However, often the standards we set for ourselves are based on unrealistic and inappropriate expectations. It's common to fault yourself for what happened, the way you reacted or failed to react, what you thought or felt or didn't think or feel.

Loss or trauma brought on by the loss of another person, whether it's through a broken relationship, divorce, or death, often moves us into a selective memory mode. We tend to remember everything that was negative in our relationship while failing to recall the positive. Initially in times of loss we tend to dwell on the negative things we contributed to the relationship and overstate the good things the other person contributed.

Guilt grows when we repeat the "if only's," "could haves," "should haves," and "shouldn't haves." I've heard statements like "I should have known CPR," "I shouldn't have let him ride that motorcycle," and "If only I'd had the radio on, I would have heard the tornado warning."

This type of reaction is especially true when the loss involves a child. For example, after the crisis of a miscarriage or stillbirth, parents question themselves and each other. They wonder if it happened because of something they did or didn't do.

When an adolescent chooses a different lifestyle or value system, a parent asks, "Where did I go wrong?" "Why didn't I spend more time with him?" "Why didn't I take an interest in his schoolwork?" "If only I had homeschooled him instead."

We may even feel guilty over some of the feelings we experience during the upset of a crisis. I've talked to many people who have said their guilt came because during their loss, they doubted God, questioned God, didn't have enough faith, didn't believe enough, or weren't spiritual enough. When guilt enters our life, whether it's realistic or exaggerated, we tend to develop an unhealthy preoccupation with how bad we are. We look at ourselves in a distorted way. We focus on our sinful state and fail to remember God's offer of forgiveness.

More and more today we hear about survivor guilt. Accidents, tornadoes, earthquakes, and terrorist attacks create a special kind of remorse in those who survive the tragic event. There were many survivors of the Oklahoma City bombing with only minor injuries or no injuries at all. Many of them experienced survivor guilt. The firemen and police officers who survived the collapse of the Trade Towers in New York talk about their sense of guilt in escaping death. There were those who didn't go to work that day or left early or went downstairs and missed the collapse of the towers. They too ask, "Why me?" but for a different reason. Even some of the family members of those who were lost in TWA Flight 800 ended up asking, "Why them? It should have been me. They were too young. I'm older." This type of questioning often happens when the tragedy involves a child or someone you know well. The belief that it would have been more sensible for the tragedy to have happened to you rather than the other person is a clear indication of survivor guilt. At the heart of these feelings could be the belief that you were allowed to avoid the tragedy at the cost of the other person. That feeling is rarely anchored in fact. Survivor guilt is another form of self-blame. It's a way of saying, "If I had suffered more, you would have suffered less."

There are two kinds of guilt. Some call them good guilt and bad guilt; others call them legitimate guilt and illegitimate guilt. Guilt that is often out of proportion to an event is the bad or illegitimate kind of guilt. Feeling this kind of guilt can be normal in a crisis that involves the loss of a significant person, and usually it comes from the unrealistic beliefs we hold, the "I should haves" that no one could ever attain.

The person who moves on in life from a trauma talks over his or her feelings with a person holding an objective outlook on the situation. If the only one you're talking to about your guilt is yourself, then remember, you are biased. A nonjudgmental person can help you look at whatever is creating your guilt feelings, whether they be acts, thoughts, or some perceived omissions.

Another person's rationality can help you evaluate your guilt and keep you from overemphasizing the negative.[1]

As you do this, you'll find your guilt diminishing over a period of time. And when the guilt creeps in, you'll be able to evict it more quickly each time it occurs. Whenever guilt becomes a part of your life, the following questions may help you evaluate it. You may find help by discussing these questions with a trusted friend.

- What is the reason for the guilt I feel? Is there something I did or didn't do? If so, what was it? Would anyone else agree that I was truly responsible?
- Is what I did wrong or contrary to God's Word and teaching in any way?
- Is this something I need to make restitution for or confess to anyone?

There may be legitimate, or good, guilt in your life. Good guilt has a purpose: It shows us where we've gone wrong and what we need to change. It can motivate us to grow. This legitimate guilt (which you could experience in a trauma) happens where there is a direct cause-and-effect relationship. When this kind of guilt happens, we can do something about it. We can admit what we've done, make restitution if possible, and above all confess it and receive God's forgiveness. Scripture shows us the feelings of a man struggling with guilt in Psalm 51:1–12 (NASB):

> Be gracious to me, O God, according to Your
>   lovingkindness;
> According to the greatness of Your compassion blot out
>   my transgressions.
> Wash me thoroughly from my iniquity
> And cleanse me from my sin.
> For I know my transgressions,
> And my sin is ever before me.

Against You, You only, I have sinned
And done what is evil in Your sight,
So that You are justified when You speak
And blameless when You judge.

Behold, I was brought forth in iniquity,
And in sin my mother conceived me.
Behold, You desire truth in the innermost being,
And in the hidden part You will make me know wisdom.
Purify me with hyssop, and I shall be clean;
Wash me, and I shall be whiter than snow.
Make me to hear joy and gladness,
Let the bones which You have broken rejoice.
Hide Your face from my sins.
And blot out all my iniquities.

Create in me a clean heart, O God,
And renew a steadfast spirit within me.
Do not cast me away from Your presence
And do not take Your Holy Spirit from me.
Restore to me the joy of Your salvation
And sustain me with a willing spirit.

Forgiveness belongs to us. It is always there. It can't be bought; we can't work for it. It's a gift.

I acknowledged my sin to You,
And my iniquity I did not hide;
I said, "I will confess my transgressions to the LORD";
And You forgave the guilt of my sin.

Psalm 32:5 NASB

If we confess our sins, He is faithful and righteous to forgive us our sins and to cleanse us from all unrighteousness.

1 John 1:9 NASB

One of the most graphic passages about guilt is in the Psalms:

59

There was a time when I wouldn't admit what a sinner I was. But my dishonesty made me miserable and filled my days with frustration. All day and all night your hand was heavy on me. My strength evaporated like water on a sunny day until I finally admitted all my sins to you and stopped trying to hide them. I said to myself, "I will confess them to the Lord." And you forgave me! All my guilt is gone.

Psalm 32:3–5 TLB

Perhaps what one person wrote can encourage us to deal with our guilt.

If only I had. . .

treated the one I loved
more kindly.

called the doctor sooner.

understood the full extent
of the illness.

not lost my temper.

expressed my affection
more frequently.

When death comes, life is
examined.

You become acutely aware of your failures
real or imagined.
You want to rectify past errors.
You wish to compensate for
the wrongs you have committed.
Some people even punish themselves
with self-destructive acts,

as if to say: "See how much I am suffering. Doesn't this
prove my great love?"

Self-recrimination becomes a way
to undo all the things that
make you now feel guilty.

And maybe you were guilty.
Perhaps you said things you
should not have said.
Perhaps you neglected to do things
you should have done.
But who hasn't?

What is past is past.
It cannot be changed.

You already have too much pain
to add to the burden of self-
accusation, self-reproach, and
self-depreciation.[2]

Remember that we are not able to react and respond in the best way or the way we want to when we're being traumatized. Our brain is just not capable of doing its best work at this time. Our judgment abilities are impacted.

Fear

One of the most common emotions we experience in trauma is fear. We're afraid that what happened will happen again or we'll always be like we are now. We're afraid we won't get over this or it will get worse or no one will really understand. Perhaps what fear does to us is best described by the following passages from God's Word:

I heard and my inward parts trembled,
At the sound my lips quivered.
Decay enters my bones,

And in my place I tremble
Because I must wait quietly for the day of distress,
For the people to arise who will invade us.

Habakkuk 3:16 NASB

Anxiety in a man's heart weighs it down,
But a good word makes it glad.

Proverbs 12:25 NASB

All the days of the desponding and afflicted
are made evil [by anxious thoughts and forebodings],
But he who has a glad heart has a continual feast
[regardless of circumstances].

Proverbs 15:15 AMP

The word *fear* comes from the Old English word *faer*, which means "sudden calamity or danger." The Hebrew word for fear can mean "dread."

Usually we can identify the source of our fears or "dreads." Anxiety, however, is fear with a high level of apprehension that's not directly related to anything specific. It can be very disturbing to experience these anxious feelings without knowing why. The anxiety or fear can cause numerous symptoms such as rapid heartbeat, ringing in the ears, loss of appetite, upset stomach, nausea, dizziness, nightmares, tightening of the throat and difficulty in swallowing, muscle pain, poor concentration, memory lapses, sweaty palms, and difficulty sleeping. There isn't a part of our bodies that can't be affected by anxiety.

Fear often brings along its close companion—worry. Worry is that uneasy, suffocating feeling that covers everything we see with a cloud of pessimism. It stirs up our minds and churns our stomachs. The root meaning of the word is "to choke or strangle." It's like racing the engine of a car while it's in neutral. Worry immobilizes us and causes us to focus on the worst possible outcome. We ask "What if?" again and again, each time making our answer a bit worse.

Worry is like fog. Perhaps you've driven in a dense fog that completely hid anything more than a few feet from your car. Fog has the ability to snarl the traffic of a major city and shut down an international airport. Yet a dense fog that covers seven city blocks to a depth of one hundred feet is composed of less than one glass of water.

In a similar way, a little bit of worry can fog up a lot of reality. It chills your outlook and makes everything look hazy, including your perception of life. It's so easy to fall into a pattern of worry. If that's where you are right now, you're not alone.

Your feelings of anxiety are normal. You're not going crazy. Although you want to know why you're experiencing these disturbing, anxious feelings and thoughts, you may not know for quite a while. Most likely you fear that the crisis that has shattered your expectations—your beliefs and your world—could happen again. For instance, the fear of "when and where and how will terrorists strike our country again?" has recently become a part of our national life. The more sudden and intense the crisis event, the more fear and anxiety you may experience as a result. It will help to keep in mind that you can't always explain why you feel the way you do. Also, your fear and anxiety will not always be with you. Help is available, and you can get relief.

Survivors are those who confront their fears, identify them, put them in perspective, and allow them to diminish slowly while they focus on positive improvement. Many have found it helpful to list all of their fears and place a check by them when they occur. It also helps to identify what you used to fear and how you overcame it.

Nothing helps one to overcome fear as much as concentrating on God's Word and committing it to memory. God can use passages such as Isaiah 41:10; 43:1; Philippians 4:6–9; and Psalm 37:1–10 to bring you the peace you are looking for. Never avoid or give in to your fears, because each time you do so, fear grows. Face fear, admit you're fearful, and then evict it.

..go I was privileged to meet a pastor's wife, the author of an inspiring article about a letter she wrote to her children. The letter expressed how she was struggling with a recurrence of cancer. In one part of the letter she talked about fear:

> Fear has knocked at my door. Sometimes in the past five days I have let fear in for awhile. It has not been good. I have thought of silly things like: I can't wear that new spring suit we just bought on sale or that lovely wool skirt we've waited six months for. Other times I think how much I want to see Kathy graduate, go off to Bible school, fall in love with the finest Christian man this world has ever seen, and then watch her walk down the aisle on her dad's arm. Then I think I want to see Kim married and settled. Finally, for sure, I would like grandchildren.
>
> But, dear children of mine, these are human thoughts, and to dwell on them is not healthy. I know one of the strongest desires God has given us is the desire to live, but I want to say to God that I trust Him in this too. My vision is so limited. These human desires are the purest on earth, but if I had even a tiny glimpse of heaven I wouldn't want to stay here. Because I am human, I do. So I have decided that I will put a "No Trespassing" sign at the entrance of the path of human desire and not let my thoughts wander down it.
>
> When fear knocks, it is my determined choice to let faith answer the door, faith that is settled on the sure promise of the Word of God.[3]

How can you accomplish this kind of settled decision? Sometimes it means asking others for help. Your fear could have a useful component to it. It could prompt you to make some necessary changes. It could be that some of your fears have value.

A conversation I recently overheard between a man and woman illustrates the healthy respect we need to have for useful fears. This couple was discussing a life-threatening experience they faced.

The man asked, "Aren't you afraid?" The woman's response was tinged with anger:

Of course, I'm afraid! What kind of person do you think I am? It isn't sensible not to be afraid when there is good reason for it. I was afraid when I was beaten as a child. I was afraid when my husband left me. I've spent a lot of my life being afraid. Show me someone who hasn't! That's why so many people resort to drugs and alcohol. It blots out their fear. There is nothing so outstanding about having fear as long as you don't act fearful—because of your fear. We've got to face our fear and move ahead.

Depression

When your trauma involves a major loss or disruption of your life, depression, the "common cold of the mind," begins to take over. It's to be expected. When hope is gone and the future looks bleak, despair finds fertile soil in your mind.

Losses are often at the heart of depression. Any loss can trigger a reactive depression—the loss of a person, a job, a home, a car, a valued photograph, a pet. The stronger the attachment, the more intense the feelings of loss. Loss is especially devastating for women because they put so much of themselves into relationships and build such strong attachments. Especially devastating is the loss of a love relationship. Maggie Scarf describes this dilemma in her classic book *Unfinished Business*:

It is around losses of love that the clouds of despair tend to converge, hover and darken. Important figures leaving or dying; the inability to establish another meaningful bond with a peer-partner, being forced by a natural transition in life, to relinquish an important love tie; a marriage that is ruptured, threatening to rupture, or simply growing progressively distant; the splintering of a love affair or recognition that it is souring and will come to nothing.[4]

Often these losses lead to a crisis, but too frequently loss is not recognized as such. We're not made aware of how losses can affect us.

The Old Testament story of Job illustrates in detail the role loss as well as trauma plays in bringing on depression. Job experienced loss to a greater degree than most of us will ever experience. He lost his wealth, his means of livelihood, his servants, and his children. Eventually he lost his own physical health and sense of well-being. He experienced the depths of depression. Listen to his complaints:

> Let the day perish wherein I was born,
>   and the night which said,
>   "A man-child is conceived."
> Let that day be darkness! . . .
>
> Why did I not die at birth,
>   come forth from the womb and expire? . . .
>
> Why is light given to him that is in misery,
>   and life to the bitter in soul,
> who long for death, but it comes not,
>   and dig for it more than for hid treasures. . . .
>
> For my sighing comes as my bread,
>   And my groanings are poured out like water. . . .
>
> In truth I have no help in me,
>   and any resource is driven from me. . . .
>
> So I am allotted months of emptiness,
>   and nights of misery are appointed to me.
> When I lie down I say, "When shall I arise?"
>   But the night is long,
>   and I am full of tossing till the dawn.
>
> Job 3:3–4, 11, 20–21, 24; 6:13; 7:3–4 RSV

No one is immune to depression, not even a Christian. Some people will experience mild depression while others dive to the depths of despondency.

The deeper your depression, the more paralyzing is your sense of helplessness. You feel passive and resigned. Everything seems out of focus. You feel as though you're in a deep, dark pit, cold and isolated. There doesn't seem to be a way out of this pit either. Depression can blind you to the realities of life. It narrows your perception of the world. You end up feeling all alone, as though no one else cares about you.

Depression affects you spiritually and can change the way you see God. It's hard to believe in a loving and personal God who knows the answers and wants you to succeed yet seems to be far off. The psalmist reflected these feelings as well:

> Lord, be kind to me because I am weak,
>> Heal me, Lord, because my bones ache.
> I am very upset.
>> Lord, how long will it be?
> Lord, return and save me.
>> Save me because of your kindness.
> Dead people don't remember you.
>> Those in the grave don't praise you.
> I am tired of crying to you.
>> Every night my bed is wet with tears.
> My bed is soaked from my crying.
> My eyes are weak from so much crying.
>> They are weak from crying about my enemies.
>
> Psalm 6:2–7 NCV

In place of experiencing peace and joy—the light of God in your life—you feel just the opposite. You feel empty. Often Christians who are depressed feel even worse because of their false beliefs about depression. *It is not a sin for a Christian to be depressed.* And most of our depression is not brought on by sin.

Many people are surprised to read the account of Jesus's depression in the Garden of Gethsemane. Jesus was perfect man and free from all sin, yet complete in his humanity and tempted as we are. Look at the account in Matthew 26:36–38 (AMP):

> Then Jesus went with them to a place called Gethsemane, and He told His disciples, Sit down here while I go over yonder and pray. And taking with Him Peter and the two sons of Zebedee, He began to show grief and distress of mind and was deeply depressed. Then He said to them, My soul is very sad and deeply grieved, so that I am almost dying of sorrow. Stay here and keep awake and keep watch with Me.

Jesus knew what was about to happen to him, and it depressed him. He did not feel guilty over being depressed, and neither should we. But our depression creates a distortion of life and intensifies any guilt feelings we have. Thus, guilt over depression leads to more depression.

Be aware, too, that if you tend toward depression even before experiencing a crisis, then your depression will be intensified during a crisis.

Look for your depression "trigger." Some triggers are obvious: You're readily aware of what prompted the depression. Other causes are more difficult to discover. To help you track them down, you may want to write the following questions on a card:

What did I do?

Where did I go?

With whom did I speak?

What did I see?

What did I read?

What was I thinking?

Refer to this card when you're depressed; it may help if you recall the thought or event that triggered the depression.

Please do not attempt to deal with your depression by yourself. Reading the recommended books may help you, but if the depression has been with you for some time, talk to a trusted friend and seek out a professional Christian counselor. But do something. The lethargy that is a by-product of being depressed causes us to behave in a way that reinforces our depression. Let me suggest what Brenda Poinsett recommends; she experienced a deep depression herself and writes about it in her book *Why Do I Feel This Way?* If you are experiencing any of the symptoms she mentions below (applicable to both men and women), please seek out someone trained in helping others with their depression:

> We need help when we don't know what caused the depression. The black cloud of despair came out of nowhere. The despair is dark and deep, and in all honesty we cannot fathom a cause.
>
> We need help if we are having suicidal thoughts.
>
> We need help if we are having delusional thoughts.
>
> We need help if we can't sleep, or we are losing a serious amount of weight, or we are experiencing severe physical discomfort in which our health may be affected.
>
> We need help if we have had repeated depressive episodes in our life.
>
> We need help when the depression is hurting our marriage, our family, or our job.
>
> We definitely need help if the depression has lasted longer than one year.

A person fitting any of these conditions needs to consider outside help in getting over his or her depression. Depression is a treatable illness. While there is no one simple cure that works for everyone, a number of treatments are available.[5]

If one method doesn't bring you out of depression, another likely will. Anyone suffering from depression needs to know how to get help and what kind of help is available.

There are times when a person will benefit the most in his or her struggle with depression by counseling or medication or both. If you experience depressive episodes frequently (daily to several times a week), with the symptoms lasting for a two-week period or longer and with intensity, you may want to seek counseling. The depressive tendency to isolate yourself may inhibit you from taking the necessary steps to get help. Don't keep your depression to yourself. Let others who are knowledgeable and caring know what your struggles are.

In many cases medication has helped to break the incessant cycle of being depressed. Medication is nothing to be afraid of or avoided. I have seen it help many people. Many different types of medication are available today. These are to be prescribed and used only under the care of a physician or psychiatrist. Some have definite side effects, and it is not uncommon for one medication to be changed to another or the dosage adjusted in order to find the right combination.

If you find yourself becoming depressed, evaluate your thoughts and value judgments. This is very important, because if your thinking pattern is negative and you persist in making negative value judgments about yourself, depression will result.

First, recognize and identify the thoughts that you express to yourself. When something happens and you experience depression, you need to realize that there is more than the outward event behind your feelings. Perhaps you had a negative thought or made a negative value judgment regarding the thing that happened. This sets you up for depression.

Second, realize that many of your thoughts are automatic. They are involuntary. You don't have to think about having them—they just pop in. They are not the result of deliberating or reasoning. But if you reason against them, you can put them aside.

Third, distinguish between ideas and facts. Just because you may think something does not mean those thoughts are true. If you are depressed because you feel that your spouse doesn't like the way you dress or the meals you cook, check with him. You may be right—but you could also be wrong. If you make an assumption, always try to see whether it is true.

Finally, whenever you discover that a particular thought is not true, state precisely why it is inaccurate or invalid. This step is vital! Putting the reasons into words helps you in three ways: it actually reduces the number of times the idea will recur, it decreases the intensity of the idea, and it tones down the feeling or mood that the idea generates. The more you counteract your negative ideas in this way, the more your depression is lessened.

Listen to your depression. There's a message in it. It's telling you that something is amiss in your life. It's like a warning system or a protective device that can keep you from further stress. Admit your feelings to another person who can help you. Don't believe the messages your depression is telling you, because depression heavily distorts reality toward the negative. Be aware that depression immobilizes you and makes you feel lethargic. You actually begin to behave in a way that will reinforce your depression. You will need to counter your feelings and do the opposite of what you're thinking, or you may not be able to behave in a nondepressed manner.

Listen to what Jane learned about her depression:

> I've struggled with this depression for ten months now. My divorce, along with the demotion at work, crushed me. Through counseling and reading I finally got to the place where I could accept my depression as normal, and I didn't feel guilty over it. One day I sat down and tried to figure out what my depression was trying to say to me. It dawned on me that the depression was a symptom, and there were causes. I began to list them. The two losses helped

to bring on my depression. So did the fact that I was rejected by my husband and at work. I was eating more to help me feel better, but it made me not like myself. So I made some plans with some friends to hold me accountable. I'm learning to grieve my losses and say good-bye to some dreams. I've learned that since I was rejected I started to reject myself. I'm no longer doing that! And I've changed my food habits. The depression is still around, but I see it lifting. Now I have the hope that someday it will leave.

If feelings of lethargy and depression have settled over you like a fog, learn as much as you can about depression. Read about it. Discover its meaning for your life. Consider what you have been through recently. Your depression is just a part of the normal array of feelings you may need to experience as you move on to recovery. Above all, keep focused on the strength of the Lord and his Word.

Those who survive are people of faith, especially faith in the promises of God. Dwell on his promises. Believe them:

Blessed are those who mourn, for they shall be comforted.

Matthew 5:4 NASB

Come to Me, all who are weary and heavy-laden, and I will give you rest.

Matthew 11:28 NASB

Blessed be the God and Father of our Lord Jesus Christ, the Father of mercies and God of all comfort, who comforts us in all our affliction.

2 Corinthians 1:3–4 NASB

When you pass through the waters, I will be with you;
And through the rivers, they will not overflow you.
When you walk through the fire, you will not be
scorched,
Nor will the flame burn you.

Isaiah 43:2 NASB

In the same way the Spirit also helps our weakness; for we do not know how to pray as we should, but the Spirit Himself intercedes for us with groanings too deep for words.

Romans 8:26 NASB

For I am convinced that neither death, nor life, nor angels, nor principalities, nor things present, nor things to come, nor powers, nor height, nor depth, nor any other created thing, will be able to separate us from the love of God, which is in Christ Jesus our Lord.

Romans 8:38–39 NASB

My grace is sufficient for you, for power is perfected in weakness.

2 Corinthians 12:9 NASB

For You light my lamp;
The LORD my God illuminates my darkness.

Psalm 18:28 NASB

The LORD is my light and my salvation;
Whom shall I fear?
The LORD is the defense of my life;
Whom shall I dread?

Psalm 27:1 NASB

Perhaps the best way to deal with emotions that invade your life is to follow the example of a hiker who had just read the Forest Service instructions of what to do when encountering wild animals, especially mountain lions. This man was jogging with his dog and came upon a mountain lion. The lion began to stalk the man and then ran after him. Fortunately, the man remembered what he had read. He stopped, turned around, and faced the mountain lion. The lion wasn't expecting this, so it stopped and walked away. Your emotions are like that mountain lion. Face them head-on, listen to their message, and eventually you'll rise above them.

Remember, you have more control over these emotions than you realize, whether it be fear, anger, sadness, anxiety, guilt, or depression. It's possible to welcome them into your life, talk with them, learn from them, and even at the moment lower their intensity. Using one of God's gifts—our imagination—see in your mind a volume dial like you would find on a radio. This is like a "feelings" dial. It has numbers on it from one to ten, from low to the most intense. Look carefully at this dial in your mind. See what it's made of. Imagine how it feels in your hand. Now select the unpleasant feeling and determine what number on your dial reflects how weak or strong it is. What number is the dial on now? What is it like to be on that number? What would it be like to be on two? On eight? Or somewhere in the middle? If you would like to turn it down, what number would you turn it to? Now turn the dial lower and lower until it goes down one number from where you started. Keep turning it down lower and lower and lower. Do it slowly until you find the intensity you want. Go slow and breathe deeply. What is it like when you reach the desired number?

Whenever your feeling intensity is too high, go through this process. When it's lower, you can handle the feelings better.[6]

When we go through a trauma, we sometimes believe that God has abandoned us. But he hasn't.

When we go through a trauma, we sometimes feel as if nothing matters. But there *are* things that matter.

When we go through a trauma, we sometimes think life is not worth living. But it is!

In times of loss and sorrow, we people of faith have to "believe against the grain." In our weakness, God reveals his strength, and we can do more than we thought possible.

Faith means clinging to God in spite of our circumstances. It means following him when we can't see him. It means being faithful to him when we don't feel like it.

Resilient people have a creed that says, "I believe!" and they affirm their creed daily. In essence they say:

- I believe God's promises are true.
- I believe heaven is real.
- I believe God will see me through.
- I believe nothing can separate me from God's love.
- I believe God has work for me to do.

"Believing against the grain" means having a survivalist attitude. Not only can we survive a crisis, but out of it we can create something good.[7]

5

The Emotions of Trauma

Grief

(NORMAN WRIGHT)

Grief—what do you know about this experience? We use the word so easily. It's the state we're in when we've experienced a significant loss, especially that of a loved one. It's an inward look. You've been called into the house of mourning. It's not a comfortable place. It's not where you want to reside, but for a time, longer than you wish, you will do just that. Often it will hurt, confuse, upset, and frighten you. It's described as intense emotional suffering or even acute sorrow.

In grief the bottom falls out of your world; the solid footing you had yesterday is gone. It feels as if the floorboards you walk on are tilting or like each step you take is into soft, pliable mud. The stability of yesterday's emotions has given way to feelings that are so raw and fragile you think you are losing your mind.

When Nicholas Wolterstorff lost his twenty-five-year-old son in a tragic climbing accident, he pictured grief as a sudden rupture of his world: "There's a hole in the world now. In the place where he was, there's just nothing. A center, like no other, of memory and hope and knowledge and affection which once inhabited this earth is gone. Only a gap remains. . . . The world is emptier. My son is gone. Only a hole remains, a void, a gap, never to be filled."[1]

Everyone has grief, but mourning is a choice. You cannot make your grief better, make it go away, fix it, or just "get over it." You need to express what is inside.

A Long, Slow Journey Called *Grief*

When you enter into grief, you enter into the valley of shadows. There is nothing heroic or noble about grief. It is painful. It is work. It is a lingering process. But it is necessary for all kinds of losses. It has been labeled everything from intense mental anguish to acute sorrow to deep remorse. As some have said, "It's a feeling of heaviness. I have this overwhelming oppressive weight which I can't shed." "Grief is an angry ocean, tossing us about like corks in the churning depths. Grief pounds us with wave after wave of emotion until our chest hurts, and we literally gasp for air. Grief pulls us into the deepest abyss of darkness and despair, until we give up hope of ever reaching shore."[2]

One man said, "This last year it's like I've been going through life like a flat tire."

A multitude of emotions is involved in the grief process—emotions that seem out of control and often appear in conflict with one another. With each loss comes bitterness, emptiness, apathy, love, anger, guilt, sadness, fear, self-pity, and helplessness.

The pain of grief can be overwhelming. It's like a visitor who has overstayed his welcome. There will be days when you want this experience to be history.

We are not immune to pain, but we resist its intrusion. There are several ways we use to do this. Some of us fight the pain through denial. We say, "No, it isn't true" or attempt to live our lives as though nothing has happened. When we hear about the loss or the tragedy, our first response is often, "No, that's not true. Tell me it isn't so!" or "No, you're mistaken." We're trying to absorb the news, and it takes time to filter through the shock. This is normal. We're trying to make sense of the nonsensical. But some continue this process of denial. When asked how they are doing, their response is always, "I'm doing just fine," instead of honestly saying, "I am really hurting today." Denial can lead to even greater losses. The author of *A Grace Disguised* said of those who are unwilling to face their pain that "ultimately it diminishes the capacity of their souls to grow bigger in response to pain."[3]

Grieving is moving through several levels of denial. Each stage brings home the reality of the loss a bit deeper and more painfully. We accept it first in our heads, then in our feelings, and finally we adjust life's pattern to reflect the reality of what has occurred. Some deal with this pain by bargaining, indulging themselves, or venting anger. But all of these are attempts to deflect the pain.

Will the Scriptures help you with your pain? Yes and no. "The Scriptures are not a medicine cabinet, filled with prescriptions to take the edge off of life. They are about a God who during his most painful experience on earth, refused the wine mixed with myrrh that was offered him."[4]

Grief Is Unpredictable

Grieving is a disorderly process. You won't control it, nor can you schedule its expression. Our friend Jane describes the unpredictable, disorderly process of grief:

> The first time I experienced grief I was lying in bed and I began to smell a terrible odor. I went into the kitchen to see if my roommate

was cooking something. Nothing. I searched fervently around the house so I could get rid of the foul odor. Nothing. As I turned off the lights and lay back down on my bed, I heard a voice (whether an angel or a demon, I don't know): "You're smelling him." In an instant, the long-forgotten memory of the first man who molested me slammed into the forefront of my mind. I gagged from the odor and from the thought of what he did to me. That night began a downward spiral. At inappropriate times, I would find myself in tears, unable to stop the flow. I could be walking down the street or simply mopping the floor, and I would erupt in grief and tears.

Your grief will take the shape of a spiral figure rather than a linear one. Grief is not a straight line moving gradually up and toward a set point. You will move forward only to return to where you were. You think you've left behind that intense pain, and your relief is so refreshing, but you will rediscover the pain again and again. Many feel as though they are losing their mind, that they're going crazy. But the "crazy" feelings of grief are actually a sane response to grief. The following examples are all symptoms of normal grief:

- distorted thinking patterns, "crazy" and/or irrational thoughts, fearful thoughts
- feelings of despair and hopelessness
- out-of-control or numbed emotions
- changes in sensory perceptions (sight, taste, smell, etc.)
- increased irritability
- may want to talk a lot or not at all
- memory lags and mental "short-circuits"
- inability to concentrate
- obsessive focus on the loved one
- losing track of time
- increase or decrease of appetite and/or sexual desire

- difficulty falling or staying asleep
- dreams in which the deceased seems to visit the griever
- nightmares in which death themes are repeated
- physical illness like the flu, headaches, or other maladies
- shattered beliefs about life, the world, and even God[5]

Grief disrupts your mind and thinking ability. Confusion moves in and memory takes a vacation.

You may find that your sense of time is distorted. Time goes too fast or too slow. Past and future collapse together. The future is hard to fathom.

Grief is slow, and you need it to be like this even though you'll probably want to rush it along. It will take longer than you have patience for.

Don't compare your loss with others and think their loss is worse or more painful than your own. The worst loss right now is your own.

Everyone grieves and heals differently. Some want to be connected to people as much as possible. Others prefer to be left alone. Some prefer to take care of their own problems, while others want assistance. One prefers activity, while another prefers just the opposite.

Grief Is Disruptive

It's not unusual to hear those in grief say, "I resent my grief. I don't want it in my life. It's too painful. I want to do a grief bypass."

A friend of ours described the disruption caused by her grief:

> I am in the midst of such a grieving process—where the bottom has fallen out of my world; the solid footing I had yesterday is gone—as I work through the reality of profound trauma and come out of a

81

long season of denial. It is shocking, unnerving, frightening. My world was seemingly perfect before, as I set about the business of being a happy little housewife with four kiddies, lots of friends, involved in church and Bible studies, leading ministries. Yet in the midst of this perceived perfection, I lived with an anger and sadness deep within my soul. Now I am in the disorderly process of grieving. I am looking at the beliefs of my youth and inviting Christ to show me His truth now. I am no longer okay with being put-together on the outside. Instead, I am more concerned with being a mess if it means fixing the brokenness inside.

Disruption, holes, confusion—the many faces of grief. If it was the death of a loved one, it disrupts your entire life schedule. And the ensuing grief doesn't just impact one part of you. It's not something you select off a rack at a clothing store to cover a portion of your body. It comes from within and doesn't leave one particle of your life untouched. It's consuming. Your body changes. Food doesn't taste the same, nor will the fragrance of your favorite flower be as intense. The frequency of tears will cloud your vision. Some experience a tightness in their throat or chest, an empty feeling in their stomach, shortness of breath, or rapid heart rate. Eating and sleeping patterns won't be the same. Some sleep and sleep, while others wish that sleep would come. Sleep is either an easy escape, or it's elusive. You try to fall asleep, but your mind and emotions seem locked on your loss. You may wake up and stay awake for hours trying desperately to sleep. Dreams or nightmares occur.

You develop a type of apathy as your behavior changes. Many say, "I'm just not myself." That's true. You won't be for some time. You may find yourself phasing out when others are talking. Your mind drifts off because it's difficult to stay focused and attentive. You feel detached from people and activities even though they're an important part of your life. What is upsetting is how absent-minded you may become. You may cry for "no apparent" reason.

It's common to lose your sense of awareness of both time and place. C. S. Lewis describes this apathy as the "laziness of grief."

Whether the death is expected or sudden, you may experience numbness. The more unexpected and traumatic the loss, the more intense your numbness will be. At first the feelings are muted, like muting the sound on your TV. The initial shock of knowing a loved one is dead puts most into a paralyzing state of shock.

Shock is like a breaker box in a house. When you have too many lines plugged into the same outlet, the electricity goes out. When you are overloaded by grief, your mind goes into a state of shock that allows you to keep going until you reset the "breakers" in your mind. This happens when you begin to experience and process the multiple emotions that hit you.[6]

Your mind fluctuates from being blank to thinking again and again about the one you lost. The person comes to mind hundreds of times. You feel as though your mind is talking to that person.

Your mind may be flooded by images you can't stop. It's as though your mind won't stop talking to the person. As this happens, begin to discover what is triggering the thoughts. Sometimes the more you try to fight them, the more they persist. Give yourself permission for them to exist, for in time they'll diminish. This process of ruminating is part of your healing and recovery. You feel especially needy at this time, almost impoverished.

Grief Produces Fear and Anxiety

The next set of common clusters is *fear* and *anxiety*. And the fears accumulate. They may come and go, or they may be a constant sense of dread. These are a common response whenever we face the unknown and the unfamiliar. They range from the fear of being alone to the fear of the future, from the fear of additional loss to the fear of desertion or abandonment.

It's common for a major loss to activate memories of earlier losses. And if those early losses weren't grieved over, the residue of accumulated pain may come back along with your current pain, and it's the same with trauma. At some point during the process of recovery, reflect on the question, "What else is there in my life that I've never fully grieved over?" Whatever your answer is, take what you've discovered during this loss and work on your other losses.

One of the causes of fear and anxiety is grief itself. It's different and intense. You've lost control of your life, and that creates fear. What worked for you before isn't working now, and this too creates fear. The higher the expectations you have for yourself, the greater your need for control; the more perfectionistic you are, the greater your feeling of loss of control and panic. Grief isn't logical. It's not predictable. And so you may be afraid of being consumed by your grief.

Grief Produces Anger

Another byproduct of grief is *anger*. It's a feeling of displeasure, irritation, and protest. In grief it's often a protest, a desire to make someone pay, to declare the unfairness of loss. Sometimes the anger is expressed like a heat-seeking missile. It can erupt suddenly. There is no warning. No alarms sound. The day has been calm, and then the missile explodes. And there is damage. Another day your anger may be expressed in silent withdrawal. It's subtle, but it's still there. But sometimes the anger is frozen. It's stuck, or it turns against you.

Grief Can Lead to Sadness and Despair

We've already mentioned that trauma can produce depression. The messy journey of grief can also lead us right into the valley of *sadness, depression,* and *despair*. When you are sad, you're yearning for the one you lost. Depression makes each day look as though the dark clouds are here to stay. Apathy blankets you like a shroud and withdrawal becomes a lifestyle. When grief leads to depression, your perspective gets distorted. Depression will alter your relationships because you're oversensitive to what others say and do. Jeremiah the prophet displayed these feelings: "Desperate is my wound. My grief is great. My sickness is incurable, but I must bear it" (Jer. 10:19 TLB).

The feeling of despair is such a major loss that the future looks dismal. A sense of hopelessness has invaded your life. Despair brings a sense of meaninglessness and worthlessness to life.

Some have said there is a "psalm for every sigh" we express. More than half of the psalms are laments. These psalms wrestle with God's presence and absence and his loyal, faithful love. You may feel what these writers said:

> You are God my stronghold.
>> Why have you rejected me?
> Why must I go about mourning,
>> oppressed by the enemy?
>
> Psalm 43:2

> Has his unfailing love vanished forever?
>> Has his promise failed for all time?
> Has God forgotten to be merciful?
>> Has he in anger withheld his compassion?
>
> Psalm 77:8–9

> You have put me in the lowest pit,
>> in the darkest depths.
> Your wrath lies heavily upon me;
>> you have overwhelmed me with all your waves.
>
> Psalm 88:6–7

Like grief, depression is a journey, but it feels more like a passage through an arid desert than a lush forest. It's a long, exhausting trek through a barren land. Others have traveled this way. The Israelites learned to know God through their desert discomfort.

In the midst of emotional despair, you too can experience the living God.

You are not alone in your sadness. Jesus himself was described as "a man of sorrows, and acquainted with grief" (Isa. 53:3 KJV). Nancy Guthrie, after the loss of two of her children, wrote, "And so it is in our sadness that we discover a new aspect of God's character and reach a new understanding of him that we could not have known without loss. He is acquainted with grief. He understands. He's not trying to rush us through our sadness. He's sad with us."[7]

It reminds us that God is present. There is never a moment that he isn't walking with us. In grief we feel isolated, alone. When we focus on that feeling, we forget that we are never, ever alone. It may help to say, "God, you say you are present. I don't feel your presence. I feel your absence. God, work on my mind so I remember that you *are* present, and in time I may feel your presence. But right now I need the knowledge."

Thoughts are not immune from grief. You may not like some of your thoughts. You would like more control of them, but that's difficult. The preoccupation you have with your loss death and your pain can occur when you're in a group, attempting to work through a business transaction, or when you're driving—which could lead to a ticket or an accident. Sometimes you may feel as though you've become obsessive with your thoughts because you can't let go of them.

Traumatic Grief

The loss of a loved one by natural death is difficult enough. But many losses go far beyond this. When a death occurs and you never had a chance to say goodbye, your grief will be more intense and last longer.

When a loved one dies suddenly of an illness no one knew about, it comes as a shock because there is no time for preparation. It's a time when many major decisions need to be made, yet the emotional surge you experience makes it difficult to make decisions. Sudden illness or death robs you of saying goodbye as well as gaining some closure in the relationship. You end up with a multitude of unanswered questions, but there's not much you can do. The trauma of sudden death also occurs when a loved one who was expected to die does so months before he or she was supposed to.

You see, the way in which our loved one died will have a powerful effect on how we grieve.

Sudden deaths, especially violent or accidental deaths, provoke our greatest shock, anxiety, and distress. Violent deaths make us feel vulnerable and fearful. Such deaths may provoke our rage or indignation at the injustice of the death. Suicide, too, has a tragic, shocking quality. Suicide may arouse unfounded guilt or a sense of failure among the survivors. Peaceful, sudden deaths, such as dying in one's sleep, seem more like a blessing, for we imagine this as an easy passage for the deceased. However, any sudden death provokes many questions, doubts and concerns. We wonder why the death happened. Who is to blame? Could it have been prevented? Sudden deaths feel unnatural. We preoccupy ourselves with "if only" ruminations in which we try to rewrite history to erase this disaster. Because we are so unprepared for loss in a sudden death, and because we usually have so much unfinished business with the deceased, sudden deaths seem to be the hardest with which to cope.[8]

There are many events that can move your grief into traumatic grief. Consider the following:

Traumatic grief *multiplies, lengthens,* and *amplifies* every aspect of the grief process. Traumatic grief is a direct response to disastrous events that threaten our own safety, security and beliefs around which we structure and order our lives. It is to these threats that we address our efforts to rebuild our shattered hopes.

Certain events are more likely to precipitate traumatic grief reactions. They share some common themes:

- Unexpected—The surprise elements stun and shock. We feel dazed and disoriented.
- Uncontrollable—The event is beyond our abilities to change it. We feel powerless and vulnerable.
- Unimaginable—The horrific elements are not familiar to our way of life. Our frame of reference does not include what we are witnessing. We feel appalled and horrified.
- Unreal—The event is too strange to process. We see but do not comprehend what we are seeing. We feel confused and disoriented.
- Unfair—We feel like victims who have done nothing to deserve this tragedy. We feel hurt, puzzled, angry, fearful.
- Unforgivable—We need to blame someone or something. What do we do with our anger, rage, and urge to punish? We feel powerless.
- Unprecedented—Nothing like this has happened before. We don't have a script to follow. We feel directionless.
- Unprepared—We haven't perceived a reason to ready ourselves for an unimaginable catastrophe. Our defense mechanisms may be inadequate to handle the demand. We feel overwhelmed.
- Uncertainty—We don't fully know the long-range effect on ourselves, our families, our jobs, our future, and the future of our offspring. We feel ambivalent and torn between hope and fear.

These events overwhelm our ability to cope. Many of them are experiences we should never have had to experience. If you have experienced these, you have been plunged into traumatic grief, which will multiply, lengthen, and amplify each part of the grief process. The response "It's too much, too overwhelming" is a common cry.

If you lost a loved one and the death was one of violence, you have other painful questions running through your mind, such as "Were they aware of what was going to happen?" or "Were they in pain?" Your mind tries to focus on the act itself.

If the death was due to murder or suicide, your grief is even greater because of your outrage over the act. Sometimes the strong desire we have for more details or wanting to see the body or the site prolongs the shock and pain.

An experience even worse is not knowing what happened. Sometimes a death leaves many unanswered questions. For some reason we seem to feel better when we have as much detail as possible, as bad as it is. Perhaps it's because it leaves less room for speculation. We often tend to think the worst.

Perhaps you had to watch a lingering death. This is an agonizing experience. It is an almost unbearable experience to see a loved one hurting, and you feel helpless to ease the suffering. You try. You ask. You plead. But you end up feeling helpless. It is hard to live with what feels like a death sentence, followed by a reprieve, followed by another horrendous bout of pain—and this may be repeated again and again during a long illness.

If you were the one who discovered the death, your grief will tend to be complicated. The scene may be frozen in your memory and difficult to let go, especially if this was not expected. All this creates extra issues for you to deal with that other family members or friends don't have to deal with. You may see others moving forward in their grief recovery sooner than you, and you may feel left behind. But your recovery will occur. Others didn't have the burden to carry that you had.

Sometimes there is no body to view or to bury, which can leave you with some doubts: "Did he really die?" "How will I know for sure?" This has happened in many types of accidents, disasters, and battles.

Recovering from Grief

Recovery—it seems like an elusive dream. It's something most grieving people desperately want but wonder if it's attainable. "When will I arrive? When will it happen?" are the concerns. It's not a one-time arrival at a set destination. It's an ongoing process. It started when you began to grieve. It has been going on for some time and will continue. Some days it seems possible, and some days you wonder.

Actually, *recovery* is not even the best word, since it means returning to the way life was before—and you can never do that. *Relearning* is a better, more accurate word choice. You will relearn your world and your place within it.

What seems strange now will begin to feel familiar. Right now one of the strongest experiences is the absence of your loved one. It's a hole with sharp, jagged edges. Over the months and years the edges dull and the absence begins to become the familiar. This, too, is a sign of relearning and recovery.

There is another side to grief. It may not be what you expect. It won't be pain-free. Life won't be back to normal. It will be different. You will create a new normal. Right now you may be feeling stuck, and it's a feeling worse than being caught in traffic where you know there will eventually be relief. It's more of being mired in quicksand where each step you try to take, you sink deeper. I've been in quicksand before. You feel trapped, and soon panic takes over. With grief it's easy to believe the numbness or pain or sorrow or anger will be your constant life companion. It won't. All that you experience will diminish. But it's like learning to swim. You have to step into the water to begin the process. It's safe on the shore because it's familiar.

The journey of grief will take you through uncharted waters. The unfamiliar, though, will become familiar. It will become your new life. And it's better than remaining frozen with grief. Grief has a beginning but it also has an end, even though it doesn't seem possible.

Everyone seems to ask, "How long will it take? How long before the grief journey is over?" After the tragic and sudden death of Susan's husband five years ago, she still cries out, "When will the pain end? God has granted me so much healing, but my heart still aches. I still miss Shawn. I wish he was here for our two boys. When will the ache feel better?" By asking these questions, Susan is certainly in good company. The psalmists and prophets asked God these same questions. We want answers. We want closure. We want to know there is an end in sight. Most want it over in weeks or at the most, months. It's more likely years. You can't compare yourself with others and their grief. Even within the same family, members grieve differently in expression, intensity, and duration.

But, as you consider the question, "How long will it take?" and the overall time frame of grief, there are specific points in time for you to be aware of:

The third month after the death is often very difficult. The shock and numbness have worn off, and by now it's difficult to deny your loss. Many say it feels just like the first twenty-four hours following the actual loss.

After six to nine months, you need to consider the relationship of your emotional and physical health. This is a time when your body's immune system may be weakened even more than the initial month. But if one does the work of grieving and doesn't postpone it or avoid it, the immune deficiency is avoidable.[9]

The first year anniversary is a difficult time. The intensity of grief and pain seems to return to the level it was immediately following the death. And you wonder, *What is wrong with me? Am I losing my mind? Won't I ever get over this?* It's a normal response. And by anticipating that this could happen, you won't question yourself as you realize this too is normal.

By the eighteenth month you may find yourself experiencing stretches of time when you may have many more good days than difficult ones. But then you wake up one morning and the sadness is overwhelming, and all you think about is the one you lost. You've hit a grief bump or detour, and this is normal. Tell yourself this is an indication of progress. It's normal. It's not a setback and it won't last long. What can you do? Handle it by doing what you would do if your loss were recent.[10]

You will hear others say, "You need to let go and move on." Their timing in such a suggestion is often off and out of sync with what you need to hear at the time. At first you may bristle at someone else telling you what to do. After all, they're not where you are. But wait, what if *you* told yourself to "pick up the pieces and get on with your life"? What would you do? Which piece would you pick up? That's where it begins, one piece at a time. What can you do today to begin moving on? What will you do tomorrow and the day after?

At some point "letting go" *will* be a step in your grief journey. We resist it because we think it means not caring anymore or blocking out the memories of our loved ones. Letting go is not the same as not caring. It doesn't mean not remembering your loved one. You want to do that. You need to, for memories are what you have left. Initially those sharp memories can be painful, but in time they begin to fade, and that in itself can be another loss.

No, letting go means taking the energy and emotional investment you had in that relationship and beginning to invest it elsewhere. It's shifting your focus. Letting go is leaving behind the person you lost in such a way that you're free to move on. To let go, you need to recognize what needs letting go. It could be regrets, unfulfilled expectations, anger, the lifestyle you used to have, or even a routine. Easy? No. Necessary? Yes. There's an insecurity in letting go but a greater security in embracing life. It's a process that may be repetitive, and some days will seem freer than others. And it occurs when *you* are ready.[11]

In this chapter, numerous issues about grief have been mentioned that exist but seem to be avoided. Perhaps it's their sensitive nature, or we're ashamed that these situations or feelings exist. Not addressing them hinders the grieving process. There's nothing hidden in our life, for God knows our thoughts as well as what we are going to say before we say it. Nothing surprises him, and he wants us to grieve.

Hopefully this picture of recovery will be your experience:

> Recovery from loss is like having to get off the main highway every so many miles because the main route is under construction. The road signs reroute you through little towns you hadn't expected to visit and over bumpy roads you hadn't wanted to bounce around on. You are basically traveling in the appropriate direction. On the map, however, the course you are following has the look of shark's teeth instead of a straight line. Although you are gradually getting there, you sometimes doubt that you will ever meet up with the finished highway. There is a finished highway in your future. You won't know when or where, but it is there. You will discover a greater sense of resilience when you know in advance what you will experience and that you're normal in your response.[12]

PART 2

Recovering from Trauma

How Do I Find Healing?

6

Telling Your Story

(MATT AND JULIE WOODLEY)

My car had just run out of gas as I (Julie) coasted into a parking lot facing a busy local highway. As I jerked to a stop, I watched in horror as three cars plowed into each other. A young woman emerged from the middle car, clearly dazed and distraught. Instinctively, I jumped out of my car and ran over the median and approached the young woman. In the midst of the chaos of twisted metal and smoke, I grabbed her arm, pulled her off the highway, and softly asked, "Are you all right?" She just stared at me with wide-eyed terror. I quickly moved the speechless young woman to the side of the road so she could sit on the curb.

While we waited for the police and ambulances to arrive, she sat on the curb weeping, screaming, and swearing. I simply sat beside her, sometimes placing my arm around her shoulder, sometimes just listening quietly and repeating, "I'm so sorry." Finally, she looked me in the eye and, with a strong Russian accent, asked, "Who are you?" "My name is Julie," I said. Staring back in amazement, she whispered, "My name is Julie too. Why are you here?" "Because God sent me to be with you," I said.

When the ambulance finally arrived and the paramedics insisted that she go to the local emergency room, Julie turned to me and said, "Please, please come with me. I need you to stay beside me." So as we drove to the hospital, I held her hand, sitting beside her. When we arrived at the emergency room, I continued to stay with her. As I sat next to her bed and assured her of my presence, she began to repeat the details of the accident. I encouraged her to keep sharing the entire story—every detail and every feeling. So she did. As she continued to share her traumatic story, ever so slowly her heart stopped racing and she felt safe again.

Julie's trauma was compressed into a few seconds of pain and fear, but for those who have experienced deep and prolonged trauma, one of the first steps on the healing path is the same: get the story out. Don't deny it or repress it. Don't try to pretend it didn't happen or that it didn't hurt you. Don't pretend that it's not affecting you today. Don't try to walk through it alone. Don't hope that it will all go away and heal if given enough time. It usually won't. Instead, move into the story of trauma and share it with God and at least one safe person.

This chapter is about telling the story of trauma. We could call it the "get it out" phase of dealing with past trauma. Somewhere on the healing path with Christ we must decide to share our story of pain without worrying about judging or being judged, without analyzing or being analyzed. We don't disguise it or disinfect it. In the presence of a loving God and safe people, we find a Savior and other people who simply weep when we weep (Rom. 12:15).

Getting Your Story Out—Why It's Not Easy

Telling our story may appear neat, logical, and easy. Actually, it's often messy, illogical, and difficult. I (Matt) like to compare it to the storage room in our basement. It's the one place in our house that holds everything that won't fit anywhere else. In other words, it's a mess. It's much easier to just shut the door, stay out of that room, and hope it organizes itself.

Most counselors know that wounded, traumatized people often deal with pain in the same way: shut the door, stay out, and don't even start the healing process. It's just too messy. Instead, when we experience trauma, it's easier to develop elaborate techniques to stuff and then flee from the pain inside. Psychologists call these techniques *defense mechanisms*, and most counselors claim that they are common and deeply rooted ways to hide our pain. This may sound incredibly obvious, but pain is painful. So if we can develop coping mechanisms that will help us roll the pain into little balls and stuff it in nooks and crannies in our heart, we'll certainly try it.

Psychologist Dr. Diane Langberg contends that traumatized people often employ three common defense mechanisms: repression, denial, and disassociation. *Repression* tries to take the painful experience and, leaving it basically intact, remove it from one's memory. Repression says, "Just forget it even happened. Take the whole experience and stuff it into some dark corner in your heart." It tries to keep the traumatic event at a distance. Repression is the least fragmenting of the three defenses, which is why it usually latches on to other defenses.

Denial says, "This is not happening," or "Well, I suppose it happened, but it didn't happen that way." Denial requires perceptual distortion. A person performs "spin control" on the bad memories, editing, revising, and disinfecting them. Unfortunately, according to Dr. Langberg, "As a result of denial, [the traumatized person] loses continuity in her experience and learns to ignore aspects of herself that are, in fact, vital to her well-being."[1]

For instance, my (Julie) friend Ellen vividly describes her valiant attempt to deny her past sexual abuse: "Outwardly, I was very cheerful and open and friendly, but none of it was flowing from my heart. In the darkest recesses of my heart, I carried pain—stark, cold, and frightened pain coming from the grief, the betrayal, and the guilt. I tried to build a wall around all the pain and keep the rest of me clean. I stuffed all my refuse there and locked it up tight."

Another friend of ours tended to deny the trauma by minimizing it. "It was hard to even think of my situation as trauma, since I've spent my whole life telling myself and others, 'Oh, it could have been worse. It wasn't really that bad.' Only now, as a thirty-something mother raising four children, am I truly comprehending that what I experienced was far from healthy. From the time I was three years old, my father physically assaulted me while my mother just watched. It lasted for years. Indeed, it was trauma, as it affected the core of my beliefs about myself, others, and about life. It has been the source of tears and mourning."

In my (Matt) experience as a pastor, I notice how often denial is the default mode of the human heart. Our hearts are just like that basement storage room: dark, unfamiliar, and frightening. Denial is the path of heart disengagement. Denial keeps the door shut and our hearts numb. And for most of us, numbness feels safer than entering the wildness of the human heart. Better to plod through life, doing our duty for God and others, disengaging our heart, anesthetizing it with addictions and busyness and performance and noise, than to enter and engage the reality of the human heart.

Unfortunately, denial works on a communal level as well. In other words, some people won't want to hear your story of trauma. It may require them to engage your heart with compassion and their own hearts with honesty. Furthermore, trauma often challenges some of our most cherished assumptions about life: (1) life is basically safe; (2) people get what they deserve; (3) life is orderly; (4) really bad things will not happen to me. Of course there is a

Christian version to this outlook on life that goes something like this: *If I follow the Lord, if I live life reasonably well and do the right "Christian things," God will arrange my life so that trauma will not hit me or my home.* But then trauma actually occurs and people avoid your story because it disrupts and discredits these cherished assumptions about life.

Disassociation is the third and most fragmenting defense mechanism. At this point the traumatized person splits off from reality and "checks out." He or she not only says, "This is not happening to me, so I'm out of here," but also, "The person suffering must not be the real me." In other words, the traumatized person cuts herself off from not only the pain but even the experience behind the pain.

From a young age, our friend Cheryl learned to disassociate. At the age of five, Cheryl, the daughter of seasoned and stoic missionary parents, was placed on a truck and shipped off to boarding school for the entire year. "As they loaded me on the truck," Cheryl told me, "I clung to my doll, and my parents told me that big girls don't cry. So I refused to cry. The sexual abuse started as soon as I arrived at the boarding school. I cried out to God for it to stop, but it never did. People who talked about God, people who had supposedly given their whole lives to God, either just used me or refused to protect me. I decided that this couldn't be happening to me. So I checked out, and then I even developed other personalities to protect me from the evil things that other people kept doing to me."

So Why Should You Tell Your Story?

For many traumatized people it's tempting to leave the defense mechanisms in place. Like sandbags in a flood, they keep the murky waters of pain away from our hearts. So why would anyone want to remove the sandbags and let the waters flow in? Isn't that just too risky and maybe even foolish? Why should we open up?

Our friend Bill lived that way for years. While working in law enforcement, Bill was brutally assaulted. The assault stirred up layers of past trauma as well—severe poverty, his father's abandonment and alcoholism, physical abuse in childhood. Bill, an able-bodied, competent employee, suddenly went into a shell of fear. Most people gave him simple and straightforward advice, such as "Just get over it" and "Move on quickly" and "Don't dwell on it." Or they gave him "Christian" versions with the same theme: "God wants you to get over it" and "God causes all things to work together for good" and "You should rejoice in everything, Bill." All of these messages had a common core: don't deal with the past. Keep the sandbags up; keep the floodwaters of trauma at bay. Why should Bill tell his story? Why should he even start to deal with the pain?

First, we tell our stories because the trauma won't go away by itself. The waves of trauma may recede like floodwaters, but like floodwaters, they also leave a path of hurt and destruction. Trauma leaves us feeling confused and broken inside, and all the pain doesn't just disappear—even with good advice and "biblical information."

One of the survivors from the high school shootings at Columbine offered wise advice to the Virginia Tech survivors: "For those of us who openly shared our thoughts, who cried, and who dealt with the pain immediately after it happened, we're not doing too bad. It still hurts, I still find occasion to cry. But those who never dealt with it find themselves unable to handle the simplest things. A fire alarm goes off, a balloon pops, or a police car drives by, and they find themselves doubled over in anguish, unable to move. . . . We all deal with these things in different ways. . . . It doesn't matter how we deal with it—as long as we do."[2]

Our friend Helen likes to use an illustration that her pastor-father often used in his sermons: "My dad used to hold up a red cup and tell us that the cup represented our heart. Then he would fill the cup with different things—water, coffee, Kool-Aid, or dirt—and bump it. Whatever was inside the cup would spill outside the cup. Likewise, when we're under any kind of stress, when our hearts are 'bumped,' the things that fill our hearts—hurt, hate, pain, joy, love, peace—will spill out. We can't help it. Well, after my dad died, and then as a teenager when I was sexually abused, my 'red cup' overflowed with pain, and it was starting to show. Life was bumping my cup, and my heart started flowing with anger and bitterness and pain—despite all my efforts to seal the top of my red cup."

Bill's cup started leaking as well. He began showing all the telltale symptoms of the continuing effects of past trauma, or post-traumatic stress disorder: flashbacks, nightmares, hyper-arousal, anxiety, numbness, and detachment. Many traumatized people can hide some of these effects, but like Helen's red cup illustration shows, eventually life bumps our hearts and we spill and leak.

Ironically, we often think that ignoring the past will make it go away. Actually, the opposite often occurs: by trying to ignore the pain, we allow our past pain to grip us even more tightly. But when we do face our pain and trauma, we can start to heal and move forward.

Even though I (Julie) worked as a Christian counselor, I still had to discover this truth for myself. For many years I was one of those people who refused to "face the unacceptable." I was frantically living as the perfect mother, pastor's wife, and Christian counselor, but because I had not dealt with my underlying unresolved trauma, I started dying on the inside. And then when I experienced another episode of profound rejection and loss, my life spiraled out of control, teetering on the abyss of despair. I slipped into a major depressive state and even stopped eating.

Unfortunately, this fresh stream of trauma tapped into a much larger raging river of trauma. A flood of old feelings and experiences came back to me; they seeped into my life—even in my dreams. I lost interest in daily activities, had trouble concentrating, and grew incredibly touchy and angry. I simply wanted to "disappear" from all the people who I thought loved me. In the next few months I became speechless—literally. I couldn't even formulate words. In three months I lost sixty pounds.

Eventually, God touched me and healed me, but I learned a profound lesson about trauma: it never stays in the past, neatly sealed off from the present. It constantly intrudes into the present, seeking some way to express itself. I tried to push down all the sadness and rage, but it kept popping up into my mind, emotions, and actions.

There's a second very important reason to tell our story: sharing the story starts the healing process. On one level, sharing your story will "lift the veil of denial, mystery, and silence that so often shrouds trauma."[3] For instance, after I (Julie) was sexually abused, I was warned never to speak of it again. The trauma became unspeakable. No one in my family or in my community wanted to mention it. I started to wonder if I was insane. Maybe I was just making it all up. Or maybe it wasn't a big deal after all. So I was sexually assaulted by people I trusted? Why can't I just get over it and move on? Everyone else seemed to move on.

But telling the story helped validate me and my perspective. I'll never forget the first time I told a counselor (she wasn't a Christian, but she provided a safe place to process my pain) about my past abuse. This old German woman pounded her fist on the table and shouted, "This should never have happened! This was wrong!" And then she held me and let me weep.

The events of the trauma—the sights, sounds, feelings, smells— can seem like the random jumble of an automobile junkyard. By sharing the story, you can start to organize the jumble of sensations, making sense out of the senselessness of it all. You also start to break the grip of denial and set your heart free to face the truth—in all its jagged beauty and pain.

For example, Dr. Carl Lindahl, codirector of the Surviving Katrina and Rita in Houston project, collected hundreds of stories from survivors of Hurricane Katrina. After listening to a middle-aged man share his story of being trapped for four days, struggling heroically to survive the trauma of a flood, Dr. Lindahl concluded: "As I listened to his story, I was overwhelmed by the power, the very simple power of this man reporting something that had happened to him. And it occurred to me at that time that in all the years I'd been collecting stories, I was never in a situation where it was more important for the people to tell [their stories] and more important for them to be heard and most important for them to be heard on their own terms."[4]

There is a simple power in telling our stories "on our own terms." After his younger brother committed suicide, a young man offered this advice: "Talk about the situation with someone you trust. Whether it's for three hours or for five minutes, just keep talking. The more I talked about my brother's suicide, the more I was forced to deal with it and get closer to overcoming it. By talking to someone I trusted, I was able to confront it with support."

Three Levels of Getting the Story Out

There are at least three levels to sharing our story of past trauma. *First*, there is the heart level. We simply acknowledge to ourselves that we're carrying pain from past events. We realize that although we have said our prayers, read books, listened to sermons, attended Bible studies, and given it time, the pain hasn't healed. We've developed sophisticated mechanisms to hold the pain at bay, but the pain keeps oozing around our defensive walls. At this level, we're simply honest about this fact. Again, we're not looking for or demanding answers or quick solutions. We just say to ourselves, "I don't understand, and maybe I should get over it by now, but my heart still aches. The distant trauma still clings to my soul and I can't shake it off."

At this stage there is a temptation to say, "I should be better. I should be further along. I should move beyond the trauma, so I'll pretend or hope that things are better." One big "should" regarding our healing is that we should not ask for help. Asking for help, crying out from our sense of need, makes us look infantile and dependent—and we all know that dependence is a sign of weakness, immaturity, and perhaps even moral or spiritual failure. Strong, mature, competent people should just deal with it and move on.

At this point, we may need to ask ourselves a simple question: Where did all of these "shoulds" come from? Besides, who am I to measure where I "should" be? Based on what criteria? And who decided that I should not cry out for help? Certainly, we don't find that advice in the Bible. To the contrary, the Bible often uses the words "cry" or "cry out" to describe how we can approach God. The original language (the Old Testament was written in Hebrew and the New Testament was written in Greek) behind these words suggests a sense of stark and raw urgency. The Psalms—the ancient prayer book of the Bible—are filled with people in trouble who cry out to God (see Pss. 120:1; 130:1; 138:3; 141:1; 142:1). And this crying out to God is often done in the context of a loving community.

Clearly, most of these "shoulds" do not help in the healing process. So at this first level of sharing our story, we should just send all these "shoulds" away from our heart. Just start from where we are, the real condition of our heart, rather than a made-up fantasy projection of where we think we should be.

Second, once we stop running into defenses and attend to our heart, we can move into the next level of getting our story out: we become totally honest with God. The Bible tells us to "walk in the light" (1 John 1:7 NIV), part of which implies that we are totally transparent with God about our sin, our brokenness, our rage, our sadness, and our hurt. All throughout the Bible Jesus is presented as a merciful Savior (the New Testament also uses the term High Priest) who has compassion on us because he has identified with us in our sin. At his baptism, in his acts of compassion and deliverance, in his willingness to touch the broken and eat with sinners, and especially in his death, Jesus Christ, the living God in human form, identifies with all of our human lot. "For by His wounds you were healed" (1 Peter 2:24 NASB), the Bible tells us. Pain from the present, hurts in the past, brokenness in the future—he knows it all not just through intellectualization but through his suffering and identification with us at the cross.

Jesus is not the kind of High Priest who will say, "Get over it! Haven't you dealt with that trauma by now? What's taking you so long? And by the way, it didn't really hurt that bad, did it?" No, when Jesus looked at the crowds of hurting people, "he felt compassion for them because they were distressed and dispirited like sheep without a shepherd" (Matt. 9:36 NASB). On the long road to recovering from past trauma, Jesus joins us as our caring older brother (Heb. 2:11) and as our merciful high priest who can "sympathize with our weaknesses" (Heb. 4:15 NASB).

This kind of identifying love frees us to live a totally transparent life. We fear transparency. What if I tell my story and God and others think I'm defective? What if they reject me because I'm weak? Trauma does make us feel weak and vulnerable: we can't just "get over it" in our own power and competency. We need outside help. But Christ does not despise the weakness of broken people. "A bruised reed he will not break, and a smoldering wick he will not snuff out" (Matt. 12:20). As a matter of fact, he specifically said that he came for the sick, not the healthy (Mark 2:17). Once we start attending to the pain in our hearts, we can also begin to confess our sin and brokenness because Jesus is a merciful, tenderhearted Savior for broken people.

Third, as we begin to tell our story to our own heart and in the presence of God, we can move to the last level of getting the story out: we find safe people who will listen to our story. At first you may find a friend, a small group, a therapy group, or a Christian counselor who will listen. Make sure you find the appropriate context for the level of sharing. For instance, most ordinary church small groups can't handle prolonged processing of past trauma from one person. These small groups are not your personal therapy groups.

On the other hand, there are safe people who will listen to your story. It's important for us to believe this, because many traumatized people vow never to let down and trust anyone again. So we walk through life refusing to let down our guard again. Sadly, these vows truncate our healing. Most vows are based in a distorted view of reality. Traumatized people realize that life and people are unsafe. That is partially true. For instance, after one of my (Julie) clients told the story of her childhood sexual abuse, she suddenly moved her hands to cover her face, cringing in fear. "Sheila, what are you doing?" I quietly asked. "I'm waiting for you to slap me in the head. Because my parents told me that if I ever mentioned the abuse, they would slap me in the face—and they made sure they fulfilled that promise."

Like Sheila, many traumatized people feel that other people or circumstances are unsafe and frightening. Eventually, as God begins the healing process in our souls, we discover that reality isn't that simple. According to the promises in the Bible, our entire life can rest in God's loving and sovereign embrace. In those loving arms there are safe people. So we encourage you to pray for and pursue relationships with safe people.

What does a safe person look like? When I (Matt) asked that question to Ellen, a young woman who had been sexually abused, she said, "I always felt safe around Julie because I know that she'd never make me feel invalidated or guilty. She's not embarrassed by trauma. Also, I know she likes me as a person, and my past experiences and my present struggles won't change that. So I had nothing to prove and nothing to lose with her. In my mind, that makes her a safe person."

God is always raising up safe people like Julie. They may be rare, but they certainly do exist.

When I (Julie) was diagnosed with cancer, Dr. Dan Allender offered the most helpful response I received from the Christian community. He heaved a long, deep sigh and then shouted, "Oh, crap! I am so sorry." Those simple words of anguish washed over me like a healing balm. I needed at least one person who would allow me to struggle and who wouldn't try to fix me. I discovered that the vows I often make—"I will never trust again" or "The world is always unsafe" or "People always judge you so I'll never open up"—are not the final word on my trauma. And they also block the flow of God's healing grace.

A Word of Caution

For most of this chapter we've been encouraging you to open up, stop living in denial, and honestly share your story with people you can trust. However, we'd also like to offer a word of caution related to sharing your story. Don't feel pressured to share your story on a certain timetable or in a certain way. Trauma expert Dr. Bruce Perry has stated wisely, "The problem with traumatic memories tends to be their intrusion into the present, not an inability to recall them. When they intrude, discussing them and understanding how they may unconsciously influence behavior can be extraordinarily helpful."[5] Dr. Perry gives the following guideline for sharing our stories: "The bottom line is that people's individual needs vary, and no one should be pushed to discuss trauma if they do not wish to do so."[6] So although we're encouraging you to share your story, you'll have to be the final judge of when and how and to whom you will open up your life in order to "get your story out."

Is It Worth the Risk?

As we face this first step, for some of you the risk of getting your story out may seem incredibly high. The trauma hurt you. You may not want to risk opening your heart to more hurt. Why not just leave it all alone and hope that time heals the wounds?

Remember, first of all, time by itself doesn't heal the wounds. At the very least, the wounds often heal like an untreated broken bone—it heals but it's always bent and painful. That's not true healing; that's just bare survival.

For example, when Heather finally made an appointment with me (Julie), her life had descended into emotional and spiritual chaos. She lives with an abusive, alcoholic husband (her second), she lacks positive friendships, she is subjected to her mother's pattern of criticism and verbal abuse, and she lives under a cloud of rejection and despair.

Unfortunately, Heather never dealt with the broken, "untreated" places in her heart. Instead, like many survivors of trauma, Heather coped by repressing and denying the past memories, memories that included a home filled with chaos, sexual abuse, and excessive drug use. She will continue to spiral downward until she faces the past, unwrapping the broken places in her heart and getting her story out.

On a more positive note, it's worth the risk because telling our story really can lead us down the healing path. Ellen is experiencing this truth. In a recent letter, she wrote to us, "One of the greatest, most loving, most magnificent things the Lord ever did for me was to break down the wall around my past and clean out the dirt in my 'red cup.' It was painful, like pouring alcohol over a cat scratch. It had to be done but it wouldn't always feel good. It was an exhausting period of my life and I cried a lot. But ever so slowly, things got better. I made peace within myself."

Finally, and most importantly, it's worth the risk because, in Jesus Christ, God is ready and able to embrace us in the midst of our pain and suffering. He actually wants to comfort us in the midst of our trauma. Of course, as we walk down this path, we'll quickly discover that healing is much more than getting our story out; it involves letting God into our story. In the next chapters we explain how we can bring God into our painful stories.

Practical Steps for Telling Your Story

Throughout this chapter we've reiterated that telling your story is the difficult but necessary starting point for your healing journey. Here are some practical steps to remember as you move forward in telling your story:

1. *Go slow.* Don't feel pressured to get it all out in one session or one conversation. The healing path usually requires a long, slow journey with many steps.

2. *Find someone you can trust.* Try out a little piece of your story and see how your listener responds. If he or she shuts you down, don't be discouraged. Sadly, some people cannot handle the pain or the jagged edges of trauma. But God knows that you are wired for community, and God will meet that need in his timing. By the way, this person may be a professional counselor, a friend, a pastor or small group leader, or even just someone else who has experienced trauma. One of the most effective methods for healing the wounds of Hurricane Katrina trauma victims involved survivors interviewing other survivors by sharing what they called "kitchen-table stories."

3. *Don't worry about the details of your story.* I (Julie) have many clients who are worried that their stories are just a chaotic jumble of details. The chronology and sensations appear confusing. I tell them, "That's okay. Just start anywhere and don't worry about 'making sense.' Often as you

111

start talking and sharing your story, the details will start to fall into place."

4. *Find a method of storytelling that fits you.* Poetry, drawing, painting, sculpture, writing, music, journaling, watching and discussing a film—there are so many ways to get the story out.

5. *Connect with a small group.* Hearing other stories of trauma and recovery will help you feel normal and help you create your own "new normal."

6. *Be patient.* Telling your story does not bring instant healing. Sometimes it may start to bring more pain to the surface as you unfreeze the memories, bringing them out of the deep freeze of denial. This is normal. But remember: you are on a new healing path. God will continue to guide the process.

7

Finding God after Trauma

(MATT AND JULIE WOODLEY)

"My first memory of life is being raped at age four. He smelled like cigarettes and furnace oil." This is the story of our friend Janeane, a survivor of multiple traumas. By the time she was ten years old, she had been molested and/or sexually misused by four males and four females, a few of them repeatedly. To make matters worse, she also experienced profound rejection and abandonment. In Janeane's words, "I was the product of an extramarital affair. My father left my mother standing in an airport with me in her arms, waving goodbye. He never returned, and she resented my very existence."

As you might imagine, the trauma and rejection deeply affected Janeane's relationship with and image of God. At one point, when she was asked to draw a picture of God, she drew God with his back toward her. "He knew everything that happened to me," she said, "but he didn't care. God came to me when I was sixteen and

113

offered me salvation, which I happily accepted by asking Christ into my heart. Yet I continued to see God as just another one of my abusers . . . all too willing to molest me and then abandon me."

Shattered Faith: The Spiritual Pain of Trauma

Janeane's story eloquently records a central issue for many trauma survivors: How do I trust and love God after the trauma? Of course this relates to other questions: Where was God when my father was abusing me? Where was God when my brother committed suicide? If God knew about the tragic accident or the hurricane, why didn't he stop it? When my buddies got blown up by a bomb, why did God take them and let me live? Why did God allow a bridge to collapse just as my brother drove on it? If God let this happen, then is God uncaring, or passive, or perhaps just plain cruel? What kind of God do I believe in? Trauma expert Judith Herman contends, "Survivors of atrocity of every age and every culture come to a point in their testimony where all questions are reduced to one, spoken more in bewilderment than outrage: Why?"[1] This is often true for those who believe in Jesus and those who do not.

The impact of trauma ripples out and produces pain in our spiritual lives. Counselor Kevin Coughlin notes, "A substantial and growing body of literature is concerned with the Spiritual aspects of recovery from Trauma. This is because the spirit has been traumatized. Whether it is a jagged, raw wound—or a cauterized numb one—the outcome is the same; a person in crisis is neither spiritually whole nor connected to their [faith] community."[2]

Another research study, an overview of the spiritual impact of Vietnam combat on veterans with post-traumatic stress disorder, concluded: "Faith that God is constantly available to respond to one's hopes, fears, anxieties, and tragedies can be shattered." This can result in a sense of spiritual alienation, which leads to "feeling abandoned by God, rejecting God, feeling that God was powerless to help and therefore unavailable, or feeling wartime pain was punishment from God."[3]

As we've mentioned throughout this book, trauma can reach down into our souls and violently uproot some of our basic assumptions about life. Take, for instance, the following statements that we usually take for granted: life is fair, the world is a safe place, people are trustworthy, relationships are mostly life-giving. Traumatic events can scramble these assumptions, and trauma also scrambles our basic assumptions about God as well. After years of continual sexual abuse, Janeane developed a distorted view of God. "The sovereignty of God was terrifying to me," she told us. "For years I lived in the fear that God was going to physically come down from heaven and rape me."

Another young woman who was severely beaten by her father had a less dramatic but equally damaging response to God: "While I believed in God, I did not like him nor want him around. I often saw God standing behind the doorway while my father beat me, and always wondered why he allowed this to happen. Eventually I stopped going to church and shoved God far away."

In the midst of this confusion and spiritual questioning, Christians are often told to believe the promises of God. "And we know that God causes all things to work together for good to those who love God, to those who are called according to His purpose" (Rom. 8:28 NASB). Of course that's easy to repeat with our lips but difficult to believe in our hearts. Quoting Bible verses doesn't always eclipse all our questions about God and toward God.

Even a brilliant, spiritually mature believer like C. S. Lewis could experience grief and loss and offer this heart-wrenching but honest paragraph:

Where is God? This is one of the most disquieting symptoms. When you are happy, so happy that you have no sense of needing Him, so happy that you are tempted to feel His claims upon you as an interruption, if you remember yourself *and* turn to Him *with* gratitude and praise, you will be—or so it feels—welcomed with open arms. But go to Him when your need is desperate, when all other help is vain, and what do you find? A door slammed in your face, and the sound of bolting and double bolting on the inside. After that, silence. You may as well turn away. The longer you wait, the more emphatic the silence will become. There are no lights in the windows. It might be an empty house. Was it ever inhabited? It seemed so once. And that seemingly was as strong as this. What can this mean? Why is He so present a commander in our time of prosperity and so very absent a help in time of trouble?[4]

So how do we rebuild our shattered faith after traumatic events? How do we believe that God is good, that he is for us in Christ Jesus? How do we trust God's good heart toward us? How do we take the jagged, raw wound in our souls and offer the pain to a Savior who claims to be our healer? In other words, how do we trust and embrace God so that Romans 8:28 becomes a reality for us?

In some ways, this chapter will be the most "theological" part of this book. But don't let that scare you away. Theology is a way to think and feel and enter into the reality of God. In particular, it's a way for Christians to find the God reflected in Scripture and in the face of Jesus Christ. More than anything, good Christian theology merely retells the large and grand and beautiful and hopeful story of what God has done and is doing and will do through Jesus and in the power of the Holy Spirit. So allow us to retell the story of God's rescue and reclamation of our shattered lives. It begins with the way it was supposed to be.

Movement 1: Original Beauty

We can't take the promise in Romans 8:28 (that God causes all things to work together for good for those who love him) and rip it out of its context. This promise belongs in a much larger redemptive story that God is and always has been weaving for his creation. Actually, it's a story that started long before we—or anything else—arrived on the scene. And it started long before abuse, war, suicide, rape, accidents, 9/11, tsunamis, or any other form of trauma even had a name.

It's a story that begins in the first verse of the Bible: "In the beginning God created the heavens and the earth." As you read through the first few foundational chapters in God's story of redemption, you'll notice three prominent themes: order, design, and goodness. Genesis 1:2 says, "Now the earth was formless and empty, darkness was over the surface of the deep, and the Spirit of God was hovering over the waters." This verse pictures a desolate, frightening, empty, howling wasteland. It's the place of chaos. But God was there, for "the Spirit of God was hovering over the waters," brooding over the earth like a mother eagle hovers over its young eaglet.[5] What a beautiful picture of God's heart and power: God brings order out of chaos.

The rest of Movement 1 unfolds the ordered pattern, design, and symmetry of creation. The story is structured around the theme of one week of six days in the following pattern:

- time: *there was evening and morning . . .*
- command: *God said, "Let there be . . ."*
- result: *And it was so . . .*
- assessment: *God saw that it was good . . .*
- time: *there was evening and morning . . .*

The entire creation story, which gradually increases in complexity, gives a sense of order and purpose.

Finally, it's also a story of God's goodness. God often pauses to delight in his created work until the climax of the story when God declares, "This is very good" or, literally translated, lovely and pleasing. On three occasions we're told "God blessed." From the very first chapter in the Bible, we see something about the fundamental nature and character of God—God is gracious. God loves to bless. God delights and even revels in his creation.

Movement 2: Our Brokenness

All of this envisions the beauty of God's original creation. At this point, you may be wondering: *What does this have to do with trauma?* And how is this connected to the faith-shattering experience of trauma? A Christian response to trauma begins where the Bible begins: God created a world without trauma, but the world as we know it is now fallen and broken. Pain, suffering, hyper-arousal, terror, tears, and disassociation—none of these existed in God's original good creation. For reasons we don't fully understand (although the Bible connects it to the radical freedom that God has given his creatures), God has allowed trauma to become a reality. But we can also say that trauma and every form of evil remind us that life ought to be otherwise. Trauma is an intrusion, a trespasser, and even a rude party crasher at the gates of God's good world.

What difference does that make for the trauma victim? It validates what everyone feels about trauma: the world should have been otherwise. Little girls shouldn't get raped. Mothers and fathers shouldn't lose their sons in war. A husband shouldn't die in a sudden auto accident. A wife shouldn't have to raise her children alone. In the words of Os Guinness, "In some definite but indefinable way, human life is not on track. . . . Is this mere wordplay? Far from it. It is a sure foundation to be human in the face of evil and suffering."[6]

Part of being human in the face of trauma is to grieve and even rage against the abnormality of suffering. Guinness tells a story about a well-known Christian leader who suffered personal trauma: his son died suddenly in a cycling accident. But with near superhuman strength, this leader summoned the courage to suppress his grief and preach eloquently at his own son's funeral. A week later, this same Christian leader had an emotional and spiritual collapse. His rugged, "superhuman" faith now lay shattered at his feet. As he visited Guinness and his friends, this man spoke not as the confident preacher but as an enraged and brokenhearted father—"pained and furious at God, dark and bilious in his blasphemy."

Surprisingly, Guinness and his friends did not rebuke him for his rage; instead, they read together the story in the gospel of John, chapter 11, where Jesus wept beside the tomb of his friend Lazarus. Three times the story records the anger of Jesus in the face of this trauma. One of the Greek words used for Jesus's rage, a word that means "furious indignation," described warhorses rearing up on their hind legs, snorting through their nostrils, preparing to charge into battle. This was the reaction of Jesus in the face of trauma. The beautiful world God had made was now bent, broken, and distorted. Eventually, Jesus's mission will cause him to conquer evil, but his initial response is to join us in our tears and our outrage.

Guinness concludes by saying, "The freedom this view gives is soul-stirring. Once you know in the depth of your soul that the world should have been otherwise, you are free to feel what it is human to feel: sorrow at what is heartbreaking, shock at what is wrong, and outrage at what is flagrantly wrong and out of joint."[7] Obviously, if we nurture and nurse our anger until it becomes wedded to our life, it will destroy us. But anger can also imply a sign that we're engaged with life, expressing outrage at the world's painful distortion and yearning for the heart of Jesus in a broken situation.

Janeane loves to point to the same story of Jesus in John 11, particularly the emotional center of the story, "Jesus wept" (v. 35):

Those two words for me give a refreshing and humble outlook on the harsh reality I was raised in . . . a world God did not intend for me. The mother I was born to fell short of the woman God intended her to be. Those who were responsible for my tiny body and spirit did not listen to God and nurture me. They did not love me. But the Son of God wept every time someone touched me inappropriately. He wept when my mother stood before a family court judge and told me she did not want me anymore. He wept for me. And, although I did not know it at the time, He wept with me as well.

So before we get to the glory of "all things work together for good," we trudge through the agony of "Jesus weeps." God-in-the-flesh stands beside traumatized people and groans. He not only weeps and groans; he also rears up like a warhorse, snorting through his nostrils, declaring war against trauma. By doing so, he gives us permission to groan and weep and even rage in the face of evil and trauma. In a Jesus-like approach to the world's trauma, the apostle Paul would say, "We know that the whole creation has been groaning as in the pains of childbirth right up to the present time. Not only so, but we ourselves [i.e., followers of Jesus] . . . groan inwardly as we wait eagerly for our adoption as sons, the redemption of our bodies" (Rom. 8:22–23).

Movement 3: The Brokenness of God

A perfect world gone awry. A broken world that groans. A God who enters our trauma and groans with us. That's part of what Christians call the gospel, the good news of a God who walks beside us through life's trauma. But this story of redemption takes an even more dramatic twist: the God who walks beside us in our trauma also suffers for us and with us in our trauma. In the person of Jesus, God enters the broken world and becomes broken for us.

For many traumatized people, the real sting of suffering is not the pain; it's the apparent rejection, abandonment, and even god-forsakenness. We are alone, starkly alone, and no one will be there for us. As theologian John Stott said, "Pain is endurable, but the seeming indifference of God is not. Sometimes we picture him lounging, perhaps dozing, in some celestial deck-chair, while the hungry millions starve to death."[8]

So is God lounging on his celestial deck chair while we suffer? Is God dozing while we endure the aftershocks of trauma? The cross of Jesus shatters that view to smithereens. On the cross Jesus personally experienced the full range of human trauma: pain, injustice, abuse, betrayal, mockery, humiliation, powerlessness, physical abuse, thirst, and finally, an untimely and premature death. We are not alone. God has written "I am with you" in his own blood.

In one of his dying gasps, Jesus screamed, *"Eloi, Eloi, lama sabachthani?"* or "My God, my God, why have you forsaken me?" (Matt. 27:46). That cry, which Jesus took from the first line of Psalm 22, is often called "the cry of dereliction." That's an accurate but shocking phrase. *Derelict* means that something is forsaken, abandoned, cast away like a dog's carcass on the roadside. Where is God? Where was God? Why does God get off the hook? Is God sitting in his lounge chair—watching, punishing, and turning his face away? No, followers of Jesus would say, "Look, there is our God . . . on a cross, suffering with us and for us." Jesus knew the dereliction of trauma. The Bible tells us, "He [Jesus] is despised and rejected by men, a Man of sorrows and acquainted with grief" (Isa. 53:3 NKJV). He has been "touched with the feeling of our infirmities" (Heb. 4:15 KJV).

Os Guinness tells another moving story about a group of African Christians who were attacked and raided by Sudanese rebels. The rebels looted the entire Dinka village. The stench of death hung in the air. Some of the villagers still lay on the ground, butchered by the rebels. Straw huts were ablaze. Crops had been burnt to the ground. But in the midst of the trauma, as an act of faith, the survivors started making tiny crosses out of crude sticks and pushing them into the ground. Guinness commented: "As followers of Jesus, in the horn of Africa, they served a God who they believed knew pain as they knew pain. Blinded by pain and grief themselves, horribly aware that the world would neither know nor care about their plight, they still staked their lives on the conviction that there was one who knew and cared. . . . No other god has wounds."[9]

So on our journey to Romans 8:28, surrendering our lives to God's good plan for those who love him, we pass through the story of the God who was broken for us. "By his wounds you were healed." First of all, this implies that I am not just a victim but a fugitive from God and an enemy of God. But Christ died for me. It also implies that Christ entered the brokenness of the world and the brokenness of my life. We love and serve and trust a traumatized God. No other god has wounds.

Movement 5: Complete Healing

Yes, in case you noticed, I did skip Movement 4 for now. We'll peek ahead to the final movement and then jump back to Movement 4.

God does more than suffer with us; God also ushers our lives into a final victory over evil. All throughout the Old Testament, the prophets ache and long for that coming day. On one of the very last pages of the Bible, the apostle John looked out on a new world, a world fully redeemed and renewed by Christ, and he said, "Then I saw a new heaven and a new earth, for the first heaven and the first earth had passed away, and there was no longer any sea" (Rev. 21:1). In John's world the sea represented the forces in the world that produce trauma. "The sea [had] become the dark, fearsome place from which evil emerges, threatening God's people like a giant tidal wave."[10] The sea created tsunamis and terror and separation and destruction. But when Christ returns to establish his kingdom, the trauma-producing waters of the sea will be no more. God will banish trauma from his new creation. For God "will wipe every tear from their eyes. There will be no more death or mourning or crying or pain, for the old order of things has passed away" (Rev. 21:4).

Movement 4: Living in the Messy Middle

The "messy middle"—that's where we live. We're not in God's original beauty; we're not in the final movement of complete healing; we're living between the times. Christ has come. Christ has died. Christ has touched our lives. Christ will come again. But for now we're coming to know the God who suffers with us and for us in our trauma. But we're still broken and living in a broken world. One day the risen Christ will wipe every tear from our eyes. Trauma—with all its terror, flashbacks, anger, guilt, and grief—will be healed once and for all. Christians are people who ache and even mourn for that day.

Aching and mourning? What does that mean and how does that help us in the midst of our own healing? After the sudden death of his twenty-five-year-old son in a tragic climbing accident, Nicholas Wolterstorff asked the same question: Why cheer tears? And who are the mourners? Here's the answer from the broken heart of a father who lost his son:

> The mourners are those who have caught a glimpse of God's new day, who ache with all their being for that day's coming, and who break into tears when confronted with its absence. They are the ones who realize that in God's realm of peace there is no one blind and who ache whenever they see someone unseeing. They are the ones who realize that in God's realm there is no one hungry and who

ache whenever they see someone starving. . . . They are the ones who realize that in God's realm there is no one who suffers oppression and who ache whenever they see someone beaten down.[11]

We not only ache, but in the midst of this "messy middle" we also continue to grow in Christ, struggling forward, letting our roots grow into the soil of Christ's love for us (Eph. 3:16–17). Like the journey of grief, the journey of spiritual growth in Christ is also unpredictable and sometimes confusing. Our friend Lisa, who was sexually abused on two occasions, shared in poetic form her struggle to grow. As you read these three poems, notice the spiritual journey that is slowly occurring in her heart.

Alone

I am alone inside
Can't find my way out
Closed up and dying
Crying, crying, crying

Bursting

Little girl heart
Loving, wishing, hoping,
Dreaming . . .
Living every moment
Bursting
With what could be.
I want her to stay with me.

Letting Go

Letting go
A rush of trust
So full of love
Nestled in your hands
Resting in your peace
Feel so much relief

Did you notice the movement from brokenness to openness to restfulness? It's never a neat line. Our hearts loop in and out of brokenness and openness until they land in a restful place. But then the pain sometimes returns and we have to learn to take our brokenness to God once again until we can rest in him.

For the follower of Jesus, none of this is just interesting theology; it's an invitation to experience the presence of Jesus in the midst of our wounds. When I (Julie) encounter deeply traumatized people, I believe strongly in the power of healing prayer. I have especially witnessed miracle after miracle in the practice of *theophostic prayer*. Theophostic prayer implies a basic form of prayer that invites the wounded person to find the healing presence of Jesus in the midst of his or her trauma. The facilitator of the ministry session asks the Lord to enable the wounded person to (1) embrace, own, and take responsibility for her emotional pain; (2) be willing to release all defenses and hindrances that the Lord exposes and that prevent her from moving toward God's purposes; (3) understand and discover and expose the lie-based causes of her emotional pain; (4) and then bring this lie to the Lord for his healing power and mind renewal.[12]

When our friend Anna came to us for healing prayer, she described her trauma in the following words: "Whenever my father was upset or frustrated or at 'wit's end,' his hands would fly at me in rage. He would beat me with an open hand, whaling on my back, arms, and legs as I curled into a ball to protect myself. My mother would often look on from a nearby doorway." As we prayed with Anna, inviting the presence of the risen Christ to enter into that painful time of trauma, I (Julie) quietly asked her, "Where is Jesus in this scene?" Through sobs of pain and joy, she cried out, "Jesus is standing in my place, taking the blows for me."

Finding God in Our Trauma—the Glory of God's Promise

As people begin to heal, experiencing the presence of Jesus in the midst of their traumatic events, they will increasingly trust in the glory of God's amazing promises for their lives. Underneath the healing of traumatized people, we have often found a gentle spring flowing with a strong belief in the sovereign purpose and goodness of God. Specifically, they were clinging to Romans 8:28. In spite of the trauma, they felt that God had "called them according to his purpose." And in spite of the pain, they knew that somehow God was causing all things to work together for good.

Dr. Tod Bolsinger claims that Romans 8:28 has had a profound impact on his spiritual life, but the first time he read this verse his parents had just announced their plans to pursue a divorce. Their news shattered his world. "I still remember trying to make sense of it. All things? Even this thing? Now notice that it doesn't say that all things are good or that bad things are really good things in disguise. This doesn't say that every gray cloud has a silver lining or that we need to always look on the bright side of things. No. This passage is not saying that all things really ARE good, but that a good God works all things for good for his people, to accomplish his purpose."[13]

The movement from brokenness to resting in God's promises doesn't come without a struggle. For instance, our friend Janeane told us, "I remember the first time that someone quoted 'all things work together for good for those who love God and are called according to his purpose.' I looked at the woman like she had sprouted a second head! It was so contrary to my experience up to that point in my life. When you've been told your whole life . . . that you're unloved, unwanted, and unworthy of respect, having someone tell you that you're loved immeasurably by God and that he has a wonderful purpose for your life just doesn't fit. But one of the most beautiful aspects of God's personality that I've discovered is his desire and ability to speak the truth of his love and purpose into our broken hearts. It's as if God sits back to think of ways to show us how true he is."

Our friend Kim would concur with this. After losing her father, a pilot in the Vietnam War, she never grieved the loss until a few years ago. But then the trauma of an abandoned little girl suddenly came rushing to the surface. However, after Christian counseling and the support of her husband and her church family, Kim said, "I feel that God is closer to me now than ever before. I think that before the trauma, I was a closet legalist. I subconsciously believed that if I 'did everything right' most of the time, God wouldn't let anything really bad happen to me. I didn't like to think or talk about hard things, and I was often afraid. I didn't know what to do for others who were hurting, because their pain scared me. I thought I trusted God, but since my faith was rarely tested, I didn't realize how much I was depending on my own strength. Now I think I see more clearly what is meant by the fear of the Lord. I no longer believe that I'm exempt from tragedy, but I also have a growing confidence that 'his faithful love endures forever.'"

Author John Piper claims that the "structure [of Rom. 8:28] is staggering in its size." So once we grasp and cling to and trust in the God who makes this staggering promise, we find real peace and security, even in the midst of life traumas. Piper continues with a moving description of what it means to live in the building of this promise:

> The infinitely wise, infinitely powerful God pledges that in this building, (God) will make *everything* beneficial to his people! Not just nice things, but horrible things too—like tribulation and distress and peril and famine and slaughter (Romans 8:35–37). . . .
>
> If you live inside this massive promise, your life is more solid and stable than Mount Everest. . . .
>
> Once you walk through the door of love into the massive, unshakable structure of Romans 8:28 everything changes. There come into your life stability and depth and freedom. You simply can't be

blown away any more. The confidence that a sovereign God governs for your good all the pain and all the pleasure you will ever experience is an incomparable refuge and security and hope and power in your life. When God's people really live in the future grace of Romans 8:28—from measles to the mortuary—they are the freest and strongest and most generous people in the world.[14]

8

Embracing Your Identity in Christ

(MATT AND JULIE WOODLEY)

The philosopher Martin Buber recounts a Jewish tale about a silly man who lost his true identity. According to Buber's retelling of this ancient story, when our "hero" woke up in the morning, he could never find his clothing. So one night he devised a brilliant solution: he would leave notes for every item of clothing to remind him where it was. The next morning he arose and found notes reading, "Your pants are on the dresser" and "Your shirt is on the table" and "Your hat is by the door." One by one he read the notes, picked up his item of clothing, and dressed himself. When he finally put on his hat, he looked around and cried out in confusion, "I've found all my clothes, but now I can't find myself. Where in the world am I?" He frantically searched in vain, but he could not find himself.

And so, the story concludes, that's the way it is with us. We can make a plan to find nearly everything in our lives, but at times we cannot find ourselves. We don't know who we are. We have lost our true and deepest identity.

What do we mean by *identity*? Christian psychologist Dr. David Benner defines it this way: "Our identity is who we experience ourselves to be—the I each of us carries within."[1] Biblically speaking, we could say that our identity is what names us. Our identity defines who or what we are in our deepest core. Sadly, trauma often fragments our identity, leaving us lost and confused about this deepest core. The trauma scrambles at least some of the basic assumptions about who we are. Like the man in Buber's tale, we can no longer find ourselves. In desperation and confusion, we cry out, "Who am I? Where in the world am I?"

The Shattering Experience of Trauma

We've already mentioned that one of the characteristics of trauma is that everyone will experience it differently (see chapter 2, point 8). Some of the thoughts in this chapter may not apply to you. However, most trauma counselors agree that trauma often affects our identity on at least three levels:

1. Trauma shatters our view of our "competence."
2. Trauma shatters our view of a "safe" world.
3. Trauma shatters our experience with community.

Assaulting Our Competence

Prior to our traumatic experience, most of us faced life with a confident expectation that we were competent people who could manage most circumstances. But trauma, because it is inherently overwhelming (to our bodies, minds, and spirits), often disrupts and even shatters this basic assumption of competence. In other words, trauma can bring us face-to-face with our inadequacy and incompetence. The title of one popular book on trauma says it all:

I Just Can't Get Over It. Spiritually speaking, prior to the trauma, perhaps we considered ourselves strong, capable, and good people. Maybe we considered ourselves mature or at least growing Christians. But then trauma struck, leaving a legacy of bitterness, fear, anxiety, shame, and mistrust that we couldn't just get over—even after quoting Bible verses, attending prayer meetings, joining a small group, and serving on a church committee.

Of course it isn't just the trauma itself; there are also normal and sometimes inevitable reactions to the trauma. Another book by a leading expert on trauma is entitled *The Body Remembers*. Trauma does that to us: it stays in our system so that even if our minds forget it, our bodies continues to store the pain. For instance, as Norman discussed in chapter 2, the experience of hyper-arousal stems from bodily systems that are simply reacting to the reality of past traumatic experiences. The experience of hyper-arousal isn't necessarily an example of sin or incompetence, but when we can't master it right away, it destroys our illusions of our strength and self-sufficiency.

Sometimes the blows to our self-worth and competence are subtle; at other times they feel like a mugging. For instance, after the trauma of physical and sexual abuse in the home of my childhood, my (Julie) self-worth felt assaulted. The blows and wounds from my abusers left a profound message on my spirit: I am ugly, stupid, and unwanted. I didn't know what to do with the pain so I started drinking, taking drugs, and sleeping with boyfriends. I just wanted to be held and loved, but my reaction to the trauma made me feel even worse. It created a vicious cycle: I was desperate for someone to give me just a drop of love, but I knew I didn't deserve anyone's love, so I descended into self-destructive behaviors. According to this cycle, I deserved exactly what I got—pain, abuse, abandonment, guilt, shame, and loneliness. I deserved it all because, deep down, I was bad, defective, and worthless.

The assault on our self-worth leaves a scar of guilt and shame. As Julie experienced, trauma can plunge us into a cycle of self-rejection, self-hatred, and worthlessness. Even if the trauma wasn't our fault, we're often stuck with the belief that we could have handled it better. I could have acted more confidently or spiritually mature. I should get over my anger and fear. I should conquer these flashbacks and hyper-arousals. I could have. I should have. Without the soothing oil of God's grace, this guilt and shame begins to bury us.

Assaulting Our "Safe" World

Prior to the trauma, most of us lived with the assumption that the world was basically a safe and orderly place. Bad things happen, but not to me or my family. So although we're surrounded by tragedy and heartache, we can sigh with relief that we're still living in the first chapter of Job, grounded by a wholesome trio of wealth, comfort, and righteousness. But then trauma strikes us or our loved ones and suddenly the world doesn't look so safe after all. Everything seems more fragile and breakable.

One trauma counselor put it this way: "You used to think that if you were careful, honest, and good, you could avoid disaster. But the trauma taught you that all your best efforts could not prevent the worst from happening."[2] As a Christian we might also say that all our hard work for God, our obedience, our knowledge of the Bible and attention to spiritual disciplines still did not prevent the trauma from striking us. Since traumatic events can happen anytime to anyone, the trauma tends to make us pull back, to move through life with less confidence and security.

Assaulting Our Experience of Community

On the one hand, the pain of trauma should drive us toward community. Now, more than ever, we need others. Unfortunately, trauma can just as easily disconnect us from authentic Christian community. Many trauma survivors report a new sense of strangeness about themselves. They feel different from other people—deficient in a way that "normal" people would never understand. The trauma has somehow cut them off from the rest of normal society and normal church life. After all, how do you explain what happened to you? How do you speak the unspeakable? You are broken and damaged. No one would understand you.

This sense of being broken and damaged cuts you off from others. Jean Vanier, a man who has worked with people suffering from profound disabilities, once said, "I have discovered that even though a person may have severe brain damage that is not the source of his or her greatest pain. The greatest pain is rejection, the feeling that nobody really wants you 'like that.' The feeling that you are seen as ugly, dirty, a burden, of no value."[3] When trauma strikes it's easy to feel that nobody really wants us *like that*. As a result, it's easier just to stay away or to remain in superficial relationships for the rest of our lives.

Taking the Identity of a Victim

Thus, when trauma strikes and shatters our world, sometimes in one terrifying moment, it can brand us and scar us for life. The messages from the traumatic event—you are broken and worthless, the world is completely unsafe, you are too strange and damaged for community—reshape our identity. They solidify at the core of our being. So the "I" we carry within has been defined by the trauma, not by Christ's presence within us. As the writer William Faulkner once said about a short story character, "With nothing left, she would have to cling to that which had robbed her, as people will."[4] So although the trauma robbed us, we cling to it anyway, allowing it to become woven into our identity.

At this point, it's easy to develop the primary identity of a victim. Something bad has happened to me. It could happen again—anytime, anywhere. Life is unfair. I'm worthless. People won't love me anymore. And there's nothing I can do about it. We become like the man that Jesus encountered who was paralyzed for thirty-eight years (see John 5:1–9). Jesus asked him, "Do you want to get well?" Initially, Jesus's query may strike us as downright cold. Of course he wants to get well. He's been an invalid for nearly forty years. What was Jesus thinking?

Unfortunately, as Jesus knew so well, we can grow roots that sink into the ground of our trauma and wrap around our pain. After all, the man in this gospel story had thirty-eight years and hundreds of opportunities to move forward with his life, but for some reason he merely focused on the difficulties around him. "Sir," he addressed Jesus, "I have no one to put me into the pool when the water is stirred up, but while I am coming, another steps down before me" (v. 7 NASB). After thirty-eight years I could imagine the man coming up with something more creative. So why didn't he? We don't know his heart, but on the surface at least, it appears that his disability defined him. He experienced himself as a victim. So Jesus struck at the roots of the man's primary identity: victimization. Jesus was gently challenging this limited and inaccurate identity.

Finding Your True Identity in Christ

As Jesus confronts our false and limited identity, he offers us a better foundation for our lives. According to the Good News that Jesus brought to us, God gives us a new identity: we are the beloved of God. The New Testament writers can't seem to say it enough:

- "How great is the love the Father has lavished on us, that we should be called children of God! And that is what we are!" (1 John 3:1).

- We received "the Holy Spirit, whom he poured out on us generously through Jesus Christ our Savior, so that, having been justified by his grace, we might become heirs having the hope of eternal life" (Titus 3:5–7).
- "In love he predestined us to be adopted as his sons through Jesus Christ, in accordance with his pleasure and will—to the praise of his glorious grace, which he has freely given us in the One he loves" (Eph. 1:4–6).
- "But God demonstrates his own love for us in this: While we were still sinners, Christ died for us" (Rom. 5:8).

As you can see, this love is free, it's lavish, and it's powerful— it changes us into God's children; it justifies us by grace; and it proves God's love for us. And God lavished us with love because he *wanted* to do it ("in accordance with his pleasure and will"). As we slowly open our hearts and minds to God's amazing love for us, his love begins to shape and reshape our identity. The essential "I" becomes not just a victim of trauma (or anything else for that matter); instead, my identity shifts to something stronger, deeper, and more hopeful: in and through Jesus Christ, the Beloved One, God has named me his beloved one as well. According to David Benner, "An identity grounded in God would mean that when we think of who we are, the first thing that would come to mind is our status as someone who is deeply loved by God."[5]

Jesus constantly lived with an identity as the Beloved of the Father. At his baptism, Jesus heard his Father say, "This is my Son, whom I love; with him I am well pleased" (Matt. 3:17 NIV). This was the essential core of Jesus's life on earth. Through times of joy and sorrow and doubt and even trauma, Jesus sometimes cried out in sorrow or pain or anger or confusion, but his core identity was never shaken: "I am the Beloved of God." Jesus's whole life was defined by his Father. Everything flowed from this foundational truth.

Trauma tends to disrupt our connection to God's love in Christ. We still feel defective, broken, and unlovable; and perhaps worst of all, we feel unfixable. The flashbacks, the hyper-arousal, the grief and anger, the doubt—these "roots" of trauma seem entrenched and unmovable. As a result, the story of *I Just Can't Get Over It* becomes *I Will Never Get Over This (and therefore God could never accept me).*

For example, for years Sheila watched her father mercilessly beat her and her siblings while her mother stood in the doorway and watched. Sheila tried to put it behind her by doing the right Christian activities, but she couldn't shed the fear and the rage inside her. So she carried not only the shame from the wounds but also the guilt from her boiling anger. Sadly, the anger kept spilling over and scalding her husband and two sons as well.

But through counseling and healing prayer, Sheila is learning to write a different story for her life. The title of this story is *I'm struggling to get over this (and by God's grace I will make progress), but for now I am still and always will be the beloved of God—and nothing can take that away.* This title matches the Bible's promise that nothing "will be able to separate us from the love of God that is in Christ Jesus our Lord" (Rom. 8:39).

Bringing Our Shame and Guilt to the Cross

So what do we do with the shame and guilt that seem to linger after a traumatic event—even when it wasn't our fault? It doesn't just go away. By its very nature, trauma creates "lose-lose" situations: choose Door A and you'll get hurt or fail; choose Door B and you'll also get hurt or fail. For instance, as I (Julie) was being sexually abused, I couldn't invent a good option. I could speak up, and my parents would beat me and everyone else would mock me, because my abusers were model citizens in our small town. Or I could stay quiet and allow the abuse to continue. For years

I knew it wasn't my fault, but I also carried the shame that I had allowed the abuse to persist. And on top of that, I still felt anger and sadness for the abuse.

When our friend Susan (see chapter 2) lost her husband in a tragic car accident, her brother Bill was driving the vehicle. Even to this day, he still beats himself with shame-based questions: *Why didn't I drive slower? Why didn't I see the other car? Why did we have to go get pizza? Why did I live instead of my brother-in-law? Why can't I get on with it and start enjoying my life?* Bill still feels guilt ("I did something wrong") and shame ("I am wrong and unfixable").[6]

Trauma survivors often report feeling a deep sense of both shame and guilt. Some counselors clearly separate these two bitter fruits of trauma. Guilt is about a real violation of God's moral law. Shame, on the other hand, is a mind-set or perception that at my core I am defective and shameful. But as you can see from both of the examples above, guilt and shame act like two boa constrictors tightly wound around our chest: it's difficult to see where one ends and the other begins—and, of course, the real crisis is that we can't breathe. Untreated and long-lasting shame and guilt suck the life out of us.

As Christians we have a marvelous opportunity to bring our shame and guilt to the cross. That can sound like a pious cliché until we unpack what it means in everyday life. As an example, remember the story of trauma that Simon Peter encountered on the night Jesus was crucified. Over a period of three years Simon, the burly, self-sufficient fisherman, slowly came to believe that Jesus was the world's Messiah and Savior. Peter rejoiced that, in Jesus, the long-awaited kingdom of God was now here. But then on the night before Jesus died, Peter watched in horror as his best friend and his Lord, his deepest hope, was captured, arrested, beaten to a bloody pulp, tortured, nailed to a Roman cross, and left out to die by crucifixion. This was real trauma.

As a result of the extreme trauma, Peter discovered something about himself that he did not like: cowardice and fear ruled his heart. He experienced both poles of the fight-or-flight response to trauma. At first, he lashed out and fought, cutting off a man's ear in an attempt to defend himself and Jesus. But later he also adopted the flight response, running and hiding in fear as someone identified Peter as Jesus's friend.

Like most trauma survivors, this creates the following crisis: I'm not really who I thought I was. I am a human being who was shattered, but then I fell apart as well—and sometimes I still fall apart with the effects of trauma. It gives the devil a chance to whisper in our ears, "Don't you see—you really are a failure? You really are just a victim and nothing more. God couldn't possibly love you or use your gifts for his glory. Look at how you still respond to that traumatic experience. It still haunts you. It still gives you flashbacks and nightmares. You still startle with fear when you should not feel fear. You really are stuck in your trauma, and you'll never be anything but a failure."

What do we say to this accusation? First of all, be gentle with yourself. The very nature and definition of trauma mean that you encountered something overwhelming and extraordinary. I remember after my wife and I (Matt) moved to Long Island, Julie was hit with two forms of cancer and had a near-tragic bicycle accident—not to mention we were also moving with four children, leaving our friends and family, leaving the new home we had built, and entering a troubled church situation. At that time a marriage counselor gave us some simple but wise advice: "Nothing could have prepared you for all the trauma and loss that you've encountered. Be gentle with each other. Be gentle with yourselves." No one has ever perfectly processed trauma—except Jesus. He lived the life we should have lived. I (Matt) find comfort in the following quote: "Patience with oneself . . . is the foundation of all progress. . . . For living things grow slowly, take their time, and have many [twists] and turns."[7]

Second, we need to distinguish between responses we can control and responses we can't control. For instance, is there anything inherently wrong or sinful about the fact that we experience hyper-arousal and therefore startle easily? Of course if the startle response keeps us from attending worship services or loving our neighbor, then it's certainly a problem. But we need to reject our tendency to view any and all symptoms of trauma as signs of defectiveness or sinfulness. It could just be your body remembering the trauma.

Third, realize that, at least in one sense, some of these horrible accusations are partially true. We aren't who we think we are. Sometimes trauma just reveals what's already hidden deep in our hearts. Do you recall the cup that Helen's father used to talk about (see chapter 6)? He said that our life is like a cup that holds the contents of our heart. Life has a way of bumping into our cup and the contents of our heart spill out. But the bumping—which could be anything from an inattentive spouse or the forty-eight-hour flu to a major traumatic incident—has a way of revealing our heart's true condition.

So all of us can confess, "Yes, I am a sinner. I am not the perfect, in-control, spiritually advanced person that I thought I was. I am worse off than I ever dared to admit." This could lead to unresolved guilt and shame. But the good news of Jesus never leaves us there. We have hope! We can know the wonder and freedom of full forgiveness. The heart of the gospel is this: Jesus lived the life we should have lived, but he also died the death we should have died. He took our guilt and our shame, all of our failures, our known sins and our unknown sins, with him when he died on the cross (see Col. 2:13–15). Because of this, the Bible declares, "Therefore, there is now no condemnation for those who are in Christ Jesus" (Rom. 8:1). This promise contains no exceptions and no escape clauses. If you have trusted in him, the condemnation from guilt or shame has been settled once and for all.

Facing Our Brokenness

Once again, at the cross of Jesus, we find our true and deep-est identity: it's not being a sinner or a failure; it's not achieving success or competence; it's being a dearly loved child of God. At the cross we discover that we are not only flawed and broken and sinful creatures; we also discover that we are loved beyond our wildest imaginations. And as we bring our shame and guilt to the cross, finding the face of love in Jesus, we can also begin to face the brokenness that trauma brings.

Trauma can bring us face-to-face with our own poverty of spirit (see Matt. 5:3). Poverty of spirit simply means an awareness of how much I need God's help and mercy. As a matter of fact, I am desperate for God's grace and power. Naturally, most of us shun and deny our poverty of spirit. But poverty of spirit also includes the promise that God's hand and heart are unspeakably generous to me in the midst of my desperation. One author has stated these twin realities (our poverty and God's generosity) this way: "There is a deeply ingrained tendency to recoil from our brokenness, to judge it as others have judged it, to loathe it as we have been taught over a lifetime to loathe it . . . [but] God meets the human condition where it stands most in need, in its poverty and brokenness."[8]

Finding God's strength in our weakness reminds me (Matt) of a recent dream. I came into Jesus's presence with my hands cupped and empty as he asked me, "Why do you always go somewhere else to fill this emptiness in your hands? Are you more full?" I looked down in shame and said, "No, I'm still so empty, dry, and desperate." With a face of compassion, devoid of shame, Jesus simply replied, "I can fill the emptiness. Come to me and let me fill your hands."

Traumatized people have already been to that place of des-peration. Trauma can quickly bring us into the advanced stages of desperation and poverty of spirit. But it also makes us ready and willing to open our hearts and receive God's gift of love and strength. It's in this sense that we experience the reality of the apostle Paul's words, "For when I am weak, then I am strong" (2 Cor. 12:10). Our weakness (the trauma and the effects of the trauma) becomes strength. God begins to reverse the power of the trauma, upending the damage, altering our destiny, transforming our legacy. What was once a source of shame now becomes a source of glory. God's glory begins to shine through the cracks and wounds of our trauma.

As a contemporary example of this biblical truth, we think of Eduardo and Juliana King. They live on Long Island where their oldest son, Jose, went to high school and college. Jose enlisted with the U.S. Army and was assigned to a striker unit in Iraq. After a six-month duty, Jose surprised his parents, his wife, and his newborn daughter with a short visit home. Then he returned to Iraq to finish his tour of duty. Jose was killed in combat on August 15, 2005.

When the military came to their door to report Jose's death, Eduardo said that it was just like a scene out of *Saving Private Ryan*. The trauma unraveled Eduardo and Juliana's world. Juliana descended into a dark tunnel of sadness and despair. Eduardo struggled to heal his broken heart and to save his wife's heart as well. After watching his wife continue to plunge into darkness, Eduardo forced himself to pray with her and to read Scriptures, especially psalms of hope and lament. In the midst of their broken hearts and broken dreams, they began to cry out to God. Ever so slowly, the light of Christ began to shine into their darkness. They began to experience the reality that the apostle Paul described nearly two thousand years ago: "But we have this treasure [i.e., the presence of Jesus Christ] in jars of clay to show that the all-surpassing power is from God and not from us" (2 Cor. 4:7). That is the hope of every believer in Jesus: out of our fragile, broken condition as "jars of clay," a treasure dwells (Jesus's life); and therefore we have within us an "all-surpassing power."

Eventually, as we heal slowly, as we bring our shame and guilt to the cross, as we allow God's strength to shine through our cracks, God will use us to bring healing to others as well. In author Henri Nouwen's words, we become "wounded healers." That's exactly what happened in Eduardo and Juliana's life. Out of their trauma, God has led them to begin a ministry called Light One's Heart Foundation. This nonprofit organization ministers to the poor, the homeless, children of veterans, and those who have been traumatized by war. Obviously, for Eduardo and Juliana, the ministry is not their identity. Nor does the ministry remove all the pain from their son's death. But their hearts swell with hope as they allow the light of Christ to shine through the broken places in their "jars of clay."

Finding our identity in Christ is a long journey. Trauma shatters and fragments our identity as the beloved of God in Christ Jesus. But you are on the pathway to healing. The Holy Spirit has promised to begin a good work in you. You may stumble and fall—a thousand times—but remember that God is faithful. He will complete the good work that he started in your life (Phil. 1:6).

9

Healing for Children after Trauma

(NORMAN WRIGHT)

When does loss begin for any of us? It begins when we're children—during those years when we're most vulnerable.

Do you remember the losses of your childhood? That's when you first became acquainted with loss, even though you may not always have identified what you experienced as loss. Because many children don't identify their losses as such, they fail to grieve over their experiences. Some childhood losses are obvious; others are less so. Some are blatant while others are subtle. Some experiences are not just a loss—they're a trauma.

Life is a continual blending of loss and gain. Some losses are necessary for normal growth. For instance, a child discovers a tooth that is starting to wiggle loose. Soon it either falls out or is pulled out. But the child learns that this loss is necessary to make room for the permanent tooth. The child loses a baby tooth but gains a permanent tooth (and sometimes a little money under the pillow). But then major losses occur—far more serious than the loss of a tooth—some of which may be traumatic to the child.

The following are the most common childhood losses, in the sequence most likely to occur in a child's life: death of a pet; death of a grandparent; a major move; divorce of a child's parents; death of a parent(s); death of a playmate, friend, or relative; debilitating injury to the child or to someone important in the child's life. Were any of these a part of your childhood experience?[1] And if so, were any a trauma?

The way we learn to handle losses in childhood impacts our lives as adults. The losses of adult life may actually be compounded by some of the unresolved losses of our childhood. These are brought into adult life like unwelcome baggage. And in time, this baggage could turn an adult loss into a crisis. Losses vary in their complexity and intensity. For instance, some children are never allowed or encouraged to grieve over the loss of their favorite pet. Instead, they're told, "Don't cry. It's just a cat," or "We'll get you a new goldfish tomorrow."

A family move can be a major loss for a child. A friend saying, "I don't want to play with you anymore" is a loss. Not making the Little League team or simply not getting to play in the big game can devastate a child. Not having a favorite dress can ruin a special day for an adolescent girl. Not getting the part in a school play can spoil an entire week for some kids. Caring adults need to see losses through the eyes of the child—not through their more hardened adult eyes.

Sometimes the loss results from an unexplained withdrawal of involvement on the part of the parents. When Ken was a child, both his parents were actively involved in all of his soccer, Little League, and school activities. But when he turned eleven, they not only stopped attending his activities, but they didn't even ask him about them. No explanation was given; he couldn't understand it and ached inside for some response on their part. But it never came. This disappointment led to a fear that *everyone will end up doing this to me*, and consequently, a sense of caution and suspicion began to develop within Ken that later affected his relationships as an adult.

More and more people enter adulthood with a sense of loss because they were children of divorce. *Newsweek* magazine estimated that 45 percent of all children will live with only one parent at some time before they turn eighteen. The results of studies on children of divorce indicate that the effects of divorce on a child are more serious and long lasting than many parents are willing to admit. And more school-age children will lose a parent to divorce than to death. Self-blame for the loss (and the resulting feelings of guilt) are higher in divorced children than they are in bereaved children.[2]

These children of divorce also tend to leave school sooner than children from stable families. In New York City, which has a very high adolescent suicide rate, two out of every three teenage suicides occur among teenagers whose parents are divorced. Many others carry a pattern of insecurity, depression, anxiety, and anger into their adult years because of the loss they experienced. Divorce results in a multitude of losses for the affected child. These include not only the disruption of the family unit, but also the possible permanent loss of one of the parents, the home, neighborhood, school, friends, standard of living, family outings, family holidays, self-esteem—and the list goes on.

When a parent dies, there is a sense of closure to the relationship and usually an opportunity to say a final goodbye. Children go through an important period and sequence of mourning. But the mourning period after a divorce is open-ended. It comes and goes depending on the involvement of the noncustodial parent. If the parent does not stay involved, the children wonder if Mom or Dad will ever come back. And if not, then *why not?* The children will question what they have done to cause this situation. They will question if the loss is permanent or temporary. The occasional birthday card, the weekly phone call, and the all-too-infrequent visits and vacations tend to keep the fantasy alive that the parent might return home.

In recent years, we've been hearing more and more about childhood physical and sexual abuse. This is not just a loss that will contaminate a child's adulthood—it's a trauma. Abuse is demeaning, it takes away the innocence of children, and it distorts their perception of adults. Victims of abuse often learn to suffer silently, having lost the love of a parent, their dreams, and their innocence. In essence, they've lost their childhood.

Another damaging childhood loss is abandonment. While it's true that some children are physically abandoned, many more children are *emotionally* abandoned. Often kids don't know why they feel so alone and rejected. Their parents may be physically present and the child's bodily needs are met—but their emotional needs are neglected. They lack nurturing, hugging, and the emotional intimacy necessary for healthy emotional development. The verbal affirmations they so desperately need are shrouded in silence. Soon they begin to think that something is wrong with them, and they carry this misperception into their adulthood. Teenagers are particularly vulnerable to parental silence because they often seem to want to be left alone, causing their parents to withdraw. But the truth is, teens need constant reassurance and their parents' love and attention.

Time after time I have seen the ungrieved losses of childhood impair an adult's ability to respond normally to life and relationships. Perhaps your own adult relationships have been affected by the losses of your childhood.

Mary was four when the abuse began. First it was with her uncle. And then one day it was her father. She didn't know what to do or what to say. She wanted to tell someone but was told not to tell. So she struggled with what to think and what to feel. Her mind took her elsewhere when it happened, and soon it became buried deep within her. It became difficult for her to trust or to get close to anyone. Mary had been wounded. She had been traumatized. It shouldn't have happened.

Jim was in his first year of high school and just starting adolescence. He was bright and ahead of where he should be in school. Life for him was good until that fateful day in March. He went to his classes in Enterprise, Alabama. Hours later he was pulled from the debris with only a few scratches after a tornado had devastated the school. Physically he would be all right but emotionally was another story. He saw two of his friends crushed to death by a wall. Jim had been traumatized.

John lived with his parents and siblings in a home with a big backyard, several large trees, and plenty of lawn for running and playing. He had several friends, but his best friend was Corby, a small mixed-breed dog. He loved to play with John. Corby would constantly try to sneak into John's room to sleep on the bed.

One day John decided to put Corby on his lap while he swung from one of the tall trees. He went up higher and higher. But then he lost his grip on Corby, and the dog plummeted off John's lap, twenty feet to the ground, bouncing off the hard base of the tree. John stopped and ran to him, but Corby was dead of a broken neck.

John stood there in shock. He thought, *No!* But no sound came out of his mouth. He wanted to cry, but he couldn't. He felt numb. He felt stunned. His mother was crying, and his siblings were upset. But he was just numbed and stunned. His mom wondered, *What's wrong with him? Didn't he care enough for his dog? Is he abnormal?* John was traumatized.

Steve sat in a chair staring at the wall. He wouldn't talk. He wouldn't respond to questions. He just sat. He stayed there for hours. Finally he began to cry. He said, "We were in the school bus riding to school. We always rode together. Some days I sat behind him. Other days he sat behind me. Today he sat in front of me. All of a sudden there was a loud noise and a big piece of metal came through the window. It hit Tommy. He was all bloody and wouldn't talk anymore. He was dead. He was dead!"

It was true. A trash truck had gone out of control on the streets of Los Angeles, hit a school bus, and killed two children. All the other children were traumatized.

Children see or experience accidents. A lunchroom worker dies of a heart attack in the presence of the children. A playmate is seriously injured during a game. Any experience like this can create trauma. But unfortunately for many children, the event that creates trauma in their lives is going home at night. Physical, emotional, and sexual abuse creates lifelong traumatic results.

We used to say that in the United States few children experience human-perpetrated disasters. The Oklahoma City bombing brought a new form of trauma, and then came the World Trade Center and Pentagon disasters of September 11, 2001. The repeated viewing of these cataclysmic events, especially the planes ramming into the towers and those shiny skyscrapers cascading down in a smoky mass of destruction and death, have virtually tattooed these images on the minds of our children. At the time, *USA Today* told of a preschool child building towers out of Legos and then crashing toy planes into them again and again, saying, "They're dead. All the people are dead."

These are the traumatic events that draw national attention. But trauma of any kind turns the life of a child upside down. Some children experience it *directly*. It happens through accidents at school, in the attacks on our crime-ridden streets, or in the midst of secret, everyday violence at home. Other children experience trauma *vicariously*. With the media's constant replaying of mayhem and chaos, our wide-eyed children take on a new identity that is now described by a newly coined term for them: "living-room witnesses."

It is not a harmless phenomenon. To children, a trauma is a wound, an ongoing, festering sore that burns frightening messages into their souls:

Your world is no longer safe.
Your world is no longer kind.
Your world is no longer predictable.
Your world is no longer trustworthy.

It's difficult enough for adults to handle this, but children don't have an adult's mental or verbal ability or the life experiences to draw upon as they attempt to cope and find comfort. A child's mind doesn't work the same way as ours; it's less sophisticated and processes information differently. The trauma brings into their lives a silence, an isolation, a feeling of helplessness. And there are warning signs that a child isn't doing well.

- He consistently doesn't want to go to school; grades drop and don't recover.
- She loses all interest or pleasure in what she used to enjoy.
- He talks about hurting or killing himself.
- She hears or sees things others don't.
- He can't eat or sleep enough to remain healthy.[3]

Trauma is a condition characterized by the phrase "I just can't seem to get over it." And it's not just for those who've been through a war. I've observed it in a father who saw his daughter fatally crushed in an accident and in women who were sexually abused as children or who experienced an abortion. I've seen it in the paramedic, the chaplain, the nurse, the survivor of a robbery or traffic accident or rape, and in those subjected to intense pressure or harassment in the workplace. And I saw it on the faces of those in New York on 9/11.

The saddest thing is to see it in a child. All parents pray it won't happen in their family.

We pray to be spared because we know that trauma is much worse than a loss. Trauma is the response to any event that shatters your safe world so that it's no longer a place of refuge. And we instinctively know that children need safety more than adults do.

Trauma makes us feel powerless. It's overwhelming for adults and life-shattering for children. If we had the ability to scan the brain of a preschool child after he's experienced a trauma, what would we see?

Witnessing a tragic event is very painful. "Children often hold their hands over their hearts to show 'where it hurts most.'" And when they draw what they feel, "many . . . draw pictures of broken or blackened hearts."[4]

If your child was traumatized, he may describe what happened over and over again to anyone who will listen.

A traumatized child may need to rebuild her entire world. Many feel their lives will never be the same. What used to be safe is no longer safe. Remember that when the traumatic incident stops, for a child *it isn't over.* A boy who lost his home in a fire said, "I don't feel like I did before. The fire burned me down inside just like it did the house."[5]

A child who has been traumatized by sexual abuse is likely to be abused again in the future. Unfortunately, this child tends to act in ways she believes will bring the abuse. She believes that more abuse is inevitable, so it's better to have some control over it when it occurs than to experience the stress of waiting for its arrival.[6]

One of the unfortunate results of childhood trauma is attachment deficit disorder. It's difficult for the child to emotionally bond with others. It's difficult for the child to respond to most social interactions. Some are inhibited or hyper-vigilant or ambivalent.

Remember that your child cannot learn when he isn't relaxed. If the trauma was recent, he could be living in a constant state of fear or anxiety. Your child may appear as though he's living in another world. He may also struggle with sudden mental pictures or memories of what happened—we call these intrusive thoughts and images.[7]

What's happening in his **brain?** His thinking process has been distorted. He will experience confusion, a distortion of time, difficulties in solving problems and in figuring out what's best to do next.

As a result of trauma, something happens in the brain that affects the way a person processes information. It affects how she (or anyone, for that matter) interprets and stores the event she's experienced. In effect, it overrides her alarm system.

This will make more sense as you think of young children in their preschool years. Are they mature in any way? Their brains are especially immature. At a time of trauma, the child's brain tissue and chemistry are actually changed by sensitization. The child's brain is malleable, and it begins to organize itself around the experience of the trauma.

A child's brain responds to a trauma through imprinting. The more extensive and frequent the trauma, the more of an imprint it leaves. What is an imprint? It's like a processing template through which new information to the brain is processed. Think of this like a valley with a large river meandering through it and several streams that feed this river. When the rains come, it's fairly easy to predict what happens to the water. It flows in a predictable manner into creeks, then streams, and then the river. But then a "one-hundred-year flood" occurs, and the creeks and streams overflow their banks and cut new pathways for the overflow of water. The streams and perhaps even the river have been altered, and now they flow in different paths. And it tends to stay that way until another intense storm disrupts the flow. An imprint occurred. Childhood trauma is the equivalent of a "one-hundred-year flood." As the storm changed the course of the river, so trauma creates new imprints on the brain. And positive or neutral information from everyday experiences may be contaminated by the trauma imprint.[8]

It's difficult for a traumatized child to regulate himself. If he was abused, it's hard for him to understand what he feels and why he acts the way he does. Traumatized children often do things that don't make sense. Why does this happen? It's because a traumatized child's brain is caught in a reactive cycle of perceived threats. And since his focus is constantly on threats, he lacks awareness of why he does what he does.[9]

Hypersensitivity can actually become wired into basic brain chemistry and bodily functions. Not only that, after a trauma occurs, some of the attention and capacities in the brain, which were originally set aside for learning other skills, may be pushed aside from their original purposes to help defend against future traumas. In subtle ways the child's brain goes on alert. It's in a *prevent trauma* mode. And after enough chronic experiences, this arousal state becomes a *trait*. The child's brain organizes around the overactivated systems to make sure the child survives. Other skills are sacrificed by their defensive posture. It's not a pleasant way to live.[10] And many of our children are living that way.

What's happening in the child's **body?** Her body is out of sync. Her heart is probably pounding. She's got nausea, cramps, sweating, headaches, and even muffled hearing. Emotionally, she's riding a roller coaster and is irritable, afraid, anxious, frustrated, and angry.

Since her alarm system is stuck, she's hyper-aroused. She could even suffer from high blood pressure, rapid heart rate or irregular beat, slightly elevated temperature, and constant anxiety. She may go through her life with her alarm button on alert, constantly on the watch for any possible threat.

What's happening in his **behavior?** The bottom line is that if a child has experienced a trauma, whether an accident, death, divorce, abuse, or whatever it might be, his parents ought to expect extremes of behavior—either over-responding or under-responding.

Either way, the child's behavior is off. She's probably slower in what she does, wanders aimlessly, is dejected, has difficulty remembering, and could be hysterical, out of control, and hyper.[11]

With physical trauma, obviously some part of the body is impacted with such a powerful force that the body's natural protection, such as skin or bones, can't prevent the injury, and the body's normal, natural healing capabilities can't mend the injury without some assistance.

Perhaps not as obvious is the emotional wounding of trauma. A child's emotions can be so assaulted that his beliefs about life, his will to grow, his spirit, his dignity, and his sense of security are significantly damaged. He ends up feeling helpless. An adult can experience this to some degree in a crisis and still bounce back. However, in trauma even an adult has difficulty bouncing back, because he'll experience de-realization ("Is this really happening?") and depersonalization ("I don't know what I really stand for anymore"). So trauma is indescribable, even for adults.

Let's break down the childhood responses and reactions by age groups. This is because children of different ages are in different stages of cognitive and emotional development when they're traumatized. The very nature of brain development causes them to respond in age-related ways. Therefore we need to know what to expect at certain ages. The following are characteristics of children who have experienced trauma. These post-traumatic stress disorder symptoms are unique to children.

Children under four years old. They tend to "forget" their trauma experiences (consciously, at least for a period of time), although a few may remember from the beginning. Those over this age do remember and tend to remember the experiences vividly, whereas adults often tend to deny reality or repress their memories. Briefly, here are the prominent characteristics:

1. Most of these kids don't experience the psychic numbing common to adults. But in the case of parental abuse, they do.
2. Most don't experience intrusive and disruptive visual flashbacks.
3. School performance usually isn't impacted in acute trauma for as long a time as adults' work performance is impacted.
4. Reenactment during play increases in frequency. Time distortions are also frequent.[12]

Children of preschool or kindergarten age. Here are the most likely post-traumatic behaviors you'll observe:

1. *Withdrawal.* This is common, since children react to a trauma with a generalized response of distrusting others. Because of their limited thinking and processing ability, they can't feel safe from experiencing hurt again. They may be struggling to make sense of what they've just learned (which is overwhelmingly negative) about the world. And they may be totally silent around others, as though they're living in their own world.
2. *Denial.* This is to be expected, including denial of the facts and of memories of the event. They may avoid certain issues or ignore certain people. Distortions are common. Some children embellish the truth or develop gaps in what they remember.
3. *Anxious attachments.* These can include clinging, whining, not letting go of parents or favorite possessions, and throwing tantrums more frequently. Attachment adjustments during this stage are somewhat common.

4. *Fears.* These could include being afraid of new situations, specific objects, strangers, or males, or being restricted or confined. Such fears could occur at home, on the playground, or in the classroom. A child may balk at talking about a specific subject or refuse to read a certain story or go to a certain place or room. Some are reluctant to go home.

If a child has problems sleeping, then fear may be the cause (the best way to avoid repetitive nightmares is to stay awake). A child may wake up frequently at night. He may be dreaming about what happened. In order to find some comfort in his life, he will likely regress to behavior that worked in earlier developmental stages.

Younger school-age children. Everything mentioned about preschool children could emerge during this stage as well. But there are some additional post-traumatic characteristics.

1. *Performance decline.* Things go downhill in schoolwork, sports, hobbies, and music. If this occurs, it could be because the child is acting out or because he is preoccupied with what transpired in his life.
2. *Compensatory behavior.* Your child begins trying to compensate for the event itself or the results. There's a purpose to this response, whether he is aware of it or not. It's his attempt to deny what occurred, to reverse it, or to gain some control or retribution. This could occur through fantasy, playing the event out with others (with a different ending), or talking it out with others.
3. *Obsessive talking.* You may end up with what some parents call a chatterbox. Your child talks nonstop. As one mother said, "He wouldn't talk about it for some time, but once he started, it was all the time, over and over again. I can't turn

him off. It seems to accelerate once he starts. When he writes something for class, he always weaves in the incident."

4. *Inappropriate expressions.* This is a common response, even with adults, since in trauma there is a separation or disconnection of the functioning of the left and right sides of the brain. Sometimes a person experiences a flood of feelings (the right side of the brain), but she has no narrative from the left side to explain those feelings. Or the actual events and story may be quite vivid, but there's no emotion at this time.

5. *Repetitive reenactments.* A child of this age plays differently from your preschooler. So expect more reenactments of the event in his play and great detail. They don't necessarily help the child in his recovery, but it's another means of expression.

What do children do when they play a compensatory or reenactment game? They may kill the perpetrator, and if you walk in on this scenario, don't put a stop to it. It's purposeful. Their play may involve acting as if life were normal, as it used to be. Or their play theme may revolve around undoing the damage.

Expect your child to exhibit such changes in behavior. These are outward signs of inner confusion. A calm, steady child may become impulsive and bounce from one thing to another. He could regress. Just remember there is a purpose to what your child is doing. He's trying, in the best way he knows how, to relieve his tension and anxiety. He's trying to get attention so he can build back his sense of security. Or, since his view of life and the world has been turned upside down, he's just trying to sort through all the wreckage.

All of the changes in behavior and reenactment are stress reducers. If the stress isn't reduced, his body will begin to keep score. Physical complaints will increase; these are symptoms of his distress. Heading the list are stomachaches, headaches, and digestive upsets. On occasion your child may use these symptoms to get attention or to avoid further stress.

Older children and adolescents. Adolescents, and those on the verge of this stage, tend to act out their distress when they have experienced a trauma. Often their acting out is purposeless and destructive. They're less apt to turn to you as a parent for help; instead, they'll turn to their peers. In addition, you may encounter the following:

1. *Self-isolation.* Often we see a teen isolating herself, using drugs or alcohol, sexually acting out, cutting school or church, running away, and getting involved in suicidal activity. Sometimes the trauma isn't recent but occurred at a young age. Yet her ability to block the event has now diminished because of the changes of adolescence. This stage of development, in and of itself, is a crisis.

2. *Decreased self-esteem.* This will be coupled with an increase in self-criticism. After all, adolescents believe they're able to control their life at this stage, and when they can't, it's devastating to them. Self-blame is one of their first choices.

3. *Acting adultlike.* Sometimes a traumatized adolescent develops an older lifestyle too rapidly. These teens are described as "too old, too fast." They take on adult responsibilities prematurely, and there's very little joy in their lives.

4. *Displaced anger.* This is the kind of anger that misses the legitimate target. Instead, innocent adults and parents usually take the hit.[13]

How can you as a parent help at a time of trauma—during and after? Children and adolescents themselves have identified what they need as well as what they *don't* need in a trauma or crisis. Here is what they've said worked:

My mom or dad
   ... allowed me to talk.
   ... showed warmth and acceptance.
   ... listened well.
   ... respected my privacy.
   ... showed understanding.
   ... made helpful suggestions.
   ... was there when I needed her/him.

When helping your child or adolescent, you would be wise to *avoid* these types of interaction after a trauma:

DON'T fall apart. Even though you are upset, stay together for your children. Falling apart tells a child or adolescent that you can't really be trusted with what they have shared with you. It's essential for you to stay in emotional control. If you know it's going to be a difficult day or you're beginning to get shaky, hand off your responsibilities to someone else. Remember, you are to take care of your children. They probably aren't coping well, and they can't take care of you. Empathy must be in balance.

DON'T speculate. Avoid sharing what you're not sure of or what isn't true. Just say, "I'm not sure, but I'll find out for you." It's a matter of trust. Don't say, "Everything will be all right" unless you are 100 percent sure you know what that means and that it really will be all right. False promises cripple your credibility.

DON'T judge. Avoid any kind of judgments at this point, whether verbal or nonverbal. Focus on the needs of your child rather than on what you think "*ought* to be or *should* have been."

DON'T interrogate. You're not an inquisitor. Constant questioning can overwhelm and push your child or adolescent into silence. When questioning, be gentle and give her time to reflect on what you've asked.

DON'T clam up. Even if you don't know what to do or say, don't withdraw. Children and adolescents need you around to support, normalize, and affirm.[14]

DON'T overreact to anger. If children have experienced trauma, their anger may turn into rage or aggression. And these feelings can be confusing and frightening to everyone. It's hard for children to lose trust in people as well as lose the order and security of life. This deep fear spawns intense frustration.

DON'T withdraw support. If children see others happily going on with their lives while their own lives are in shambles, resentment builds, and some of the people in their lives may respond as if nothing happened to them. Their experience and pain need to be acknowledged. Most individuals who have experienced a loss also experience a secondary loss: when the cards and support stop coming. When this happens, they can't help but wonder if others have stopped caring, since the pain continues after the support stops.[15]

Here's the flip side of the coin. You can respond in positive ways and offer practical help when your child needs it the most:

DO encourage emotion. Some of your child's angry expressions may not be acceptable, of course (you can't let him break all the windows in your house or burn down the back porch). But it's important not to overreact and cause your child to begin stifling his feelings. Here are some suggestions. A child can

- talk it out
- write it out
- act it out in a pantomime
- sing it out
- draw it

- whisper it
- count to 57 in sets of 3 and 4 (for example, 3, 7, 10, 14, 17—this takes some thought!)
- use exercise: running in place, hopping on one foot, hitting a tetherball, etc.

If your child is shouting his anger at you, tell him you want to hear him, but it's easier for you to hear when he talks slower. Give him some guidelines:

- It's all right to feel angry.
- It's *not* all right to hit others.
- The goal is *controlled* release of anger.
- Ask: "Where is the anger in your body?"
- Ask: "What does anger look like on your face?"

Debra Whiting Alexander, author of *Children Changed by Trauma*, offers verbal prompts that parents can use to draw children out in conversation. She says:

> When there's been a crisis or trauma, it's important to help children feel free to speak their minds and to voluntarily tell you about their experiences of what happened. Never force or pressure them to tell you anything they are not yet willing to verbalize. Once they feel safe and comfortable, they may want to share with you what they went through. Here is a list of what you can say to support children who are ready to tell you their story.
>
> If you as the parent have also experienced this same event, someone else may be needed to talk with your child as well as with you. But someone needs to talk in this manner:
>
> - It's often helpful to talk about what happened.
> - Talking about what happened can help you let go of painful thoughts and memories.

- Draw a picture of what's in your mind. Write a story about what's in your mind.
- Thoughts cannot make bad things happen or prevent them from happening.
- I can handle whatever you would like to tell me about. Your thoughts don't scare or worry me.
- Anything you think about is normal for what you have been through.
- How do you imagine you might think about this in the future? in one week; three months; five years; when you're a grown-up?
- Having frightening thoughts does not mean you are going crazy. What happened was crazy; you are not.
- The trauma is over. You have survived the pain it caused, and with time you will survive the memory, too.
- It's important to talk about what you're going through and what you've been through when you are ready.
- What is your understanding of what happened?
- What do you know about it?
- What do you want to know?
- What do you wonder about it?
- Where were you when it happened?
- What were you doing?
- How did you hear about it?
- Who was involved? Who else was there?
- What did you think about when it happened?
- What did you say to yourself?
- What do you remember seeing, hearing, smelling, touching, and/or tasting?
- What most concerned you?
- What's your most painful moment or memory?
- What was your first reaction?
- What's not being talked about?
- Are other people right or wrong about what they're saying happened?
- What was handled well?

- Who was helpful and why?
- All of your thoughts before, during and after the event are normal.[16]

DO give them opportunities for creative expression. Children who have difficulty verbalizing their feelings may find it easier to express them on paper. Drawing helps kids gain control over their emotional pain and eventually eliminate it. When the loss is a death, drawing is especially important, because it allows children to actually see what their feelings look like. That helps give them a sense of understanding and control.

Writing or journaling also helps with children whose writing skills are developed. It's easier for kids to express on paper the reality of what's happened, along with their fantasies about it. Writing a letter to the deceased person—or even to God—can do wonders. Encourage your children to read aloud and discuss what they've written. But remember to respect their privacy; the choice needs to be theirs.

Encourage them to express their thoughts, fears, and feelings creatively. For example:

- Draw a picture of Grandpa.
- Sing a song about Melissa.
- Write a letter to Dad, and ask Jesus to make sure he gets it.
- Write a book about Grandma.
- Tell Fido (or Dolly) about Justin.
- Help me remember what Fluffy looked like.
- Talk to God about Aunt Emily.

DO correct their myths. It's important to discover whether your children are practicing magical thinking. Younger children are particularly vulnerable to this. For instance, your child may have argued with a friend who three hours later was killed in a car accident. Now your child may feel responsible. One young girl told her dog to "drop dead"—and the next morning it did! She thought she made it happen. Identify and correct such myths as soon as possible.

DO allow your children to respond in their own ways. Don't expect your kids to respond as you do. Initially, they may not seem upset or sad. Young children may even have difficulty re-membering the deceased. You may need to help them remember their relationship with the deceased before they can resolve their grief. Showing photos and videos will help, as well as reminiscing about times spent together.

DO normalize the reactions. Keep in mind that a trauma can change a child's life forever. It's as though she gets on a roller coaster, but this one never stops. It's like having a nightmare when he's not asleep. And the experiences change from day to day. One day the event comes back in vivid color, the next day it's black-and-white, the next day she doesn't remember it, and the next day she's numb. This all comes packaged with the fears "I'll never be the same again," "What if it happens again?" and "I'll be left all alone."

What can you say to your child when they tell you their life has been ruined by what happened to them? You could respond with, "Yes, I can see where you would feel like that. I would too. But life is more than what happened. It's a part of it, and it feels really big right now, but it's not all of it. It's sad and even tragic, but this is not your whole life."

You can try drawing this word picture for your child: Imagine holding a book and your whole life is written on all the pages inside. Imagine that those pages of your life are filled with every experience you've ever had up to today. Now, where in this book would you find the scariest experience you've ever seen or heard about or been through? This one experience is one of the many pages of memories you've had in your life. Turn to this scary page and look at it, and now let's skip to a happier time in your life. Tell me about this. You see, the scary experience (trauma) is not all of the book. It's just a portion.[17]

The best approach you can take is to love, comfort, and offer reassurance that you're there for your child. You *normalize* his reactions and feelings. Here's how you might say it:

> "I'm wondering if all your feelings are kind of confusing. That's normal. You're not going crazy. What *happened* was crazy."
>
> "You know, you're going to feel off balance for a while. It's like trying to stand on one foot. That's all right.
>
> "There's nothing wrong or weird or bad about your feeling this way. Any person—child or adult—would feel the same after something like this. It will be helpful to tell me what you need and how I can help."
>
> "Sometimes it's hard to talk about your feelings. We'll work together and find some easier ways to let them out."[18]

DO encourage. What do children need most in a post-trauma situation? Many of them need to be encouraged just to be patient with themselves. And most of all, they need to know it's all right to feel and express feelings.

DO return to childhood. Attempt to return traumatized children to the world of childhood as soon as possible. They need the routine of school, recreation, bedtime, sports, church, clubs, parties, and the like. A child responds better when he regains the environment that gives him back the security of the routine. A child needs to be given the permission to be a child again.[19]

If you don't see progress, don't hesitate to take your child to a skilled therapist who understands children's trauma. There is hope.

10

Becoming a Healing Church

(MATT AND JULIE WOODLEY)

During one of our recent worship services, a man fainted and started experiencing heart attack symptoms. With competence and compassion, our people flew into action. Two doctors, a nurse, a physician's assistant, and an EMT all converged on the man to offer help. The worship leader quietly prayed and maintained a spirit of calm. The ushers quickly brought a wheelchair and moved the man to the awaiting ambulance. Although we had never rehearsed this scenario, everyone seemed to know what to do. We proved that we can handle physical trauma.

I'd like to say that we handle emotional trauma with just as much competence and compassion. Unfortunately, for most churches, that's not always the case. For instance, after Susan's husband died, for a while we "converged" on her in the midst of trauma. People in the church brought meals, put her name on the top of their prayer list, and sent cards. But after a few months, as the

165

crisis abated, everyone went their way, leaving Susan to fend for herself. So although her freezer was still stuffed with baked ziti, her heart ached for someone to listen to her. Even four years later, she would tell me, "It's like everyone still knows that Shawn died, but no one wants to deal with it. People talk *about* it but they never talk *to* me. I just wish someone would say, 'It still must be hard. Can we do anything for you or the girls?' Instead, everyone just stays away."

Susan's story repeats itself in churches across the world. How do we bring Christ's healing to the traumatized? How do we form a community that loves and stands beside the brokenhearted? This is the profound challenge and opportunity that trauma offers to the church.

Our Challenge and Opportunity: Be the Church

On the one hand, traumatized people desperately need a safe community. In the midst of a busy, fractured, competitive world, our hearts ache for a place of refuge, a place where we can be loved in all our brokenness and vulnerability. But at times, churches can overwhelm us with programs, information, advice, and busyness. Deep down in our hearts, we long to experience the church as a vital and safe community flowing with Christ's powerful, liberating love.

Traumatized people especially need a healing community. Even secular trauma experts realize the need for community in the healing process. "Recovery can take place only in the context of relationships," writes Judith Herman in her classic work on trauma.[1] After extensive research with those traumatized by rape or war, Dr. Charles Figley developed a five-phase treatment for those who suffer from post-traumatic stress disorder. Figley's research shows that the trauma of one person affects the entire family. In other words, when one person hurts, the whole family hurts. So the first phase of his recovery model involves every family member in the healing process, not just the trauma victim. The family looks at the pain and faces the challenge together.

Another trauma expert, Dr. Peter Levine, recounts the story of his teaching assignment at a school for Hopi Indians in Mesa, Arizona. Levine made numerous attempts to encourage his students to open up and share their experiences of trauma. But after prying and prodding, he kept meeting a wall of resistance. Finally, one of his students reluctantly verbalized the problem: when they experience pain and trauma, it affects everyone in the tribe. They can't share pain merely as individuals. And thus, the healing of one person becomes the responsibility of the whole group.

Levine's and Figley's perspectives are merely restating the New Testament vision of Christian community. After telling us that we (as followers of Jesus) form one body in Christ, the apostle Paul contends, "If one part [of this body] suffers, every part suffers with it" (1 Cor. 12:26). In this vision for Christian community, the weaker members (i.e., the hurting, the brokenhearted, and the traumatized) are even called "indispensable" to the body (see v. 22). We are one body. So when one member has been traumatized by war or rape or sexual abuse, the entire body suffers trauma. As a church family, we'll look at the pain and face the challenge together.

But once again, our churches aren't always prepared for this. Like the rest of the world, it's much easier to live in denial. It's safer to keep saying, "That would never happen here, not to our people anyway." But trauma can explode anywhere. For instance, on October 2, 2006, a thirty-two-year-old delivery man entered a one-room schoolhouse in Lancaster County, Pennsylvania, took hostages, and then killed three girls before killing himself. Two additional victims died early the next morning. This traumatic incident occurred in a small Amish community in rural Pennsylvania. Suddenly, this peaceful town, sitting among rolling farmland, was scarred forever. As the body of Christ, we must jettison the illusion that our community is safe and sanitized from trauma. On any given Sunday, there's a good chance that someone with a broken, traumatized heart sits within ten to twenty feet of you.

So how do we provide a safe place for those who have been traumatized? Fortunately, we don't have to concoct a brand-new strategy, because the answer is the church. Not the church as a mere institution with bricks and budgets, but the church as the body of Christ, a living organism that continually draws life from Jesus and gives life to others in Jesus's name. And as the body of Christ, the Bible provides a beautiful way to bring Christ's life and healing to the traumatized. We just have to start being the church. Or to put it another way, in the power of the Spirit we practice the "one another" commands sprinkled throughout the New Testament. In particular, we believe that the following "one anothers" are effective ways to embrace traumatized people: accept one another, weep with one another, and serve one another.

Accept One Another

What do traumatized people need the most? Here's how Helen summarized her story of trauma and recovery: "In a nutshell, this is a story of a little girl who lost her daddy and then she lost her innocence through sexual abuse. And it's the story of a young woman who wants nothing more than to feel safe, and to know that she is loved and accepted."[2] According to psychologist Aphrodite Matsakis, Helen has expressed a core heart-cry of the traumatized: "In a society that values self-confidence and self-control, trauma survivors find themselves in a position of outsiders because they have known misery, their self-confidence has been eroded and they have trouble controlling traumatic reactions."[3] The church should be the place where "outsiders" are embraced and accepted as insiders, even in the midst of their broken past and difficult present.

And here's where the command for Christians to "accept one another" becomes so powerful. In Romans 15:7 we're given a clarion call for acceptance: "Accept one another, then, just as Christ accepted you, in order to bring praise to God." We tend to think of acceptance as the weak and passive side of love. But the Bible actually views acceptance as a strong and active form of initiating Christlike love. The Greek word for Christlike acceptance meant to welcome someone enthusiastically and practically. For instance, in one biblical scene, after Paul and his companions were shipwrecked and forced to flee to the small island of Malta, we're told, "The islanders showed us unusual kindness. They built a fire and welcomed [or accepted] us all because it was raining and cold" (Acts 28:2).

That's a beautiful picture for followers of Jesus to accept one another. Trauma is like getting shipwrecked by life. We've been thrown into the sea and pounded by the waves; we feel cold, wet, confused, and far from God. At this point, we usually don't need someone to enter our life with a lecture: "Would you just hurry up and get over it." No, we need someone who can build a fire and show us unusual kindness. That's acceptance.

Notice that acceptance isn't passive. It doesn't wait for the other person; instead, it's active, robust, and entirely Christlike. After all, in terms of our relationship with God, we were all like shipwrecked sailors clinging to a piece of driftwood, hoping that someone would come and rescue us. We needed someone to plunge into the sea, pull us out of the murky waters, drag us back to shore, and warm us by the fire. Spiritually speaking, that's what Christ did when he lived and died for us. And now that I'm accepted in Christ— even when I was unacceptable—I give glory to God by accepting others. In other words, when we accept one another, when we invite others to join us by the fire and warm their weary souls, it displays (however imperfectly) something of Christ's marvelous acceptance of us.

Acceptance is critical because trauma survivors often experience "secondary wounding." The original trauma damaged their bodies and souls, but then as they attempt to reenter the community, rejection pounds them with another wave of wounding. This nonacceptance comes in many forms:

- denial ("It didn't happen.")
- discounting ("It wasn't that bad.")
- blaming ("It must have been your fault.")
- ignorance ("It may have happened but I'd rather not know about it.")
- generalization ("Oh, you're one of *those* people.")
- or cruelty ("You don't belong in our group, so get lost.")

For a trauma survivor, any of these forms of rejection produce more pain or "secondary wounding."[4]

These examples of secondary wounding may sound extreme, but many trauma survivors can sense these attitudes from a mile away. As a simple example, when I (Julie) went for the short bicycle ride that landed me in the emergency room (see chapter 2), one of the most frequent comments I heard was, "Well, I can't believe you weren't wearing a bike helmet!" I could never gather the energy to explain that we had just moved and the helmets were still packed in storage; besides, I didn't need a lecture about bicycle safety. That comment fell under the form of secondary wounding called blaming. More than anything, I just needed a safe place to heal.

On the other hand, the church as the body of Christ can also demonstrate the beauty of Christlike acceptance. My (Matt's) friend Steve, a Christian counselor who specializes in trauma recovery, told me, "When we as the church start accepting brokenhearted people, loving them where they are and not where they 'should' be, the church will explode with growth and spiritual vitality. We'll give people freedom to work on their problems rather than feeling shame for having problems. I'm also convinced that when the church just accepts people where they are, we're providing the therapy that most people pay me for."

Weep with One Another

"Weep with those who weep" (Rom. 12:15 NASB). As a pastor, I (Matt) view this compact, simple command to be one of the rare jewels of church life. "Weep with those who weep." In our pragmatic, efficient, driven church life, I can almost hear the complaints: *That's it? Just weep with those who weep? You mean, I'm not supposed to say something, fix something, control someone, bring something, produce something? I just sit there and weep with the weepers?* And the answer is yes. Some people call it the "ministry of presence." You just show up, stay present and attentive, and then when necessary you cry or hug or pray. But there aren't any scripts. You have to trust the Holy Spirit in each circumstance and for each conversation.

One trauma survivor, a young man whose younger brother committed suicide, commented, "My friends were amazing. They made sure I didn't spend too much time by myself. After I returned to college, they remained in constant contact with me. Most of all they told me they loved me and they sat and cried with me, which I know is difficult for men. I believe that the best thing a church can do to help the traumatized is to follow the Holy Spirit and be there for hurting people with tears, open arms, open ears, and prayer."

One young woman expressed her longing for a "ministry of presence" in the following short poem:

Don't criticize.
Don't analyze.
Don't even try to sympathize.
Don't say you understand because you don't.
Just hold me in your arms for once.
And love me as I am.

Like my mommy used to do
Before the world grew up on me.[5]

Many people can administer CPR and the Heimlich maneuver, but simply weeping with the traumatized seems overwhelming. In the story of Job, for instance, after wave upon wave of trauma crashed on Job's life, when his friends initially came and saw him, "they began to weep aloud. . . . Then they sat on the ground with him for seven days and seven nights. No one said a word to him, because they saw how great his suffering was" (Job 2:12–13). Notice that they did three things right: (1) they wept with him; (2) they stayed with him; (3) they were silent before him. They were far less helpful, however, when they opened their mouths to spin their explanations and arguments. Sometimes the best "advice" and the best "answers" are silence, presence, and tears.

As a church community, we have a powerful resource for walking and praying our way through the devastation of trauma—it's called *lament*. In the act of lament, we name our grief before God and with God. But most biblical laments were written for the community, not just individuals. Laments are God's gift to train us in the art of standing with broken people. In other words, lament helps us rediscover the lost art of weeping with those who weep.

Nearly one-third of the Psalms are laments. God even gave us one jagged-edged, tearstained book devoted to the art of lament— it's called Lamentations. It begins with an agonizing cry: "How deserted lies the city, once so full of people!" As one rescue worker wandered the streets of New Orleans after Hurricane Katrina, viewing houses with markings to tally the dead, he noticed an eerie parallel between his situation and the trauma recorded in Lamentations.

Laments invite grieving people to express their pain before God and the community. It hurts, so let it out. If you want to cry or vent or shake your fist, go ahead. We're not leaving—and neither is God. Laments are an invitation to come to God and the community with our pain, rather than hide in a dark corner of anger, hurt, and bitterness. God will even provide the script (for examples of lament in the Bible, see Pss. 6, 10, 13, 22, 61, 44, 80, 88, and 102). Without laments, recovering from trauma gets short-circuited. And according to author and songwriter Michael Card, "Our failure to lament also cuts us off from each other. If you and I are to know one another in a deep way, we must not only share our hurts, anger and disappointments with each other . . . we must also lament them together before the God who hears and is moved by our tears. Only then does our sharing become redemptive in character. The degree to which I am willing to enter into the suffering of another person reveals the level of my commitment and love for them."[6]

In their work with trauma victims in Africa, the World Evangelical Alliance has discovered the value of laments. After teaching on trauma and biblical laments, one of the most powerful moments occurs when the participants write and share their own laments. Here's part of a lament written by a traumatized African woman whose home and life were ravaged by rebels:

> Eternal God, see what has happened to me.
> My soul is beaten down inside of me.
> And I don't know what to do.
> All that I built during the years is destroyed . . .
> As simply as if someone turned over a glass of water on
>   the ground.
> Come to my rescue, Lord. Come and deliver us.

Look at all these evildoers who are enjoying our goods.
They looted our house, they took our goods . . .
My throat is tight.
My heart bleeds, when I see our situation.
I don't understand why in one wink I lost everything.
Look, Lord, at all the evil that is killing me.
How long will you leave me in this situation?[7]

Rather than driving us away from God, laments keep our hearts connected to God—even as we wrestle with our feelings toward him. And as we allow people to lament, we actively welcome traumatized people into our church family. It gives them a "voice." We can begin by showing up and, like Job's friends, staying with people, weeping with those who weep, reading and singing and shouting the laments scattered throughout the Bible.

Serve One Another

We can also be a church that heals the wounded by serving one another. The apostle Paul led us into the heart of Christian community when he simply said, "Serve one another in love" (Gal. 5:13). Serving involves us in doing something. It's a gift of time and energy. Some of this can come in practical, hands-on ministries of mercy—bringing meals, calling to encourage someone, driving people to small groups or appointments. But for most traumatized people, the most practical way we can serve others occurs when we listen to their stories of trauma.

When Jesus heard the cry of a blind man (see Mark 10:46–52), he stopped. He stopped to ask a question and then to listen. How often do we simply stop and listen? My friend Denis Haack recently asked, "When was the last time someone really listened to you? I don't mean merely sat quietly waiting for their turn to talk—but truly listening? . . . They proved their willingness to enter your world, with all its brokenness, even if it cost them. Can you think of a more meaningful expression of love? If you can't remember such a time, doesn't your heart ache for it?"[8]

We all ache for someone to listen to our heart, but this deep need is even more pronounced for those who have been traumatized. The very nature of trauma is that it's overwhelming and extraordinary and therefore uncomfortable. Society (and often the church) gives a clear message: don't talk about it, at least not *here* and not *now*—maybe later, much later. "The ordinary response to atrocities," contends Judith Herman, "is to banish them from consciousness. Certain violations of the social compact are too terrible to utter aloud: this is the meaning of the word unspeakable." She speaks of the central conflict of trauma and recovery: the will to deny traumatic events versus the will to proclaim them and seek healing. "When the truth is finally recognized, survivors can begin their recovery. But far too often secrecy prevails."[9]

Churches can reverse the secrecy by creating an "unspeakable-free" zone. In other words, churches can create the context for people to talk about their atrocities. How do we do this? We stop and listen. Pastors and the spiritual leaders of the church simply say, "So tell me your story," and then we stop long enough to listen. Again, this isn't an easy act of servanthood. For instance, after my friend Joe's son died in Iraq, Joe struggled with his unspeakable pain. On some days his heart seethes with rage and an abyss of sadness. On other days he wants to declare his hope in Christ. Like many Christians, he's conflicted: he believes he should feel and act a certain way, but at the same time his story still includes chapters of grief and anger and doubt—and they won't just go away.

As the community helps Joe heal, it will require someone to serve him with the gift of listening. Or as Judith Herman wrote, "Sharing the traumatic experience with others is a precondition for the sense of a meaningful world. . . . The response of the community has a powerful influence on the ultimate resolution of the trauma. Restoration depends, first of all, upon public acknowledgment of the traumatic event and, second, upon some form of community action."[10] In other words, the Christian community stands ready to say, "Tell me your story. I will listen long enough for you to get it out. Nothing will be unspeakable here." And then after we listen we also add two more statements: (1) It happened and we are sorry. (2) We will provide a safe place for you.

Practical Steps for the Healing Church

So how do we bring all of this into the everyday life of a church? It's easy to talk about the "one anothers" as an abstract practice; but when God calls us to love, it always leads to practical, down-to-earth action. As the apostle John reminded us, "Dear children, let us not love with words or tongue, but with actions and in truth" (1 John 3:18).

Teaching

Pastors, preach the gospel. Lead us into the presence of a sovereign, merciful God who has become our Abba Father. Lift up Jesus, the one who can save and heal our broken hearts. Lead us in the power of the Holy Spirit, the one who convicts us of our sin and empowers us to live for Jesus. In the midst of church life, meeting needs and addressing hurts, don't forget to preach the gospel, the Good News about Jesus. Tell us that we're sinners and not just victims. Tell us that God is faithful even when we struggle. Tell us that Jesus died to release the captives. Tell us that a day is coming when God will wipe every tear from our eyes. Tell us and then tell us again (because we forget so easily). Preach the gospel to the lost and preach the gospel to the saved. Self-help principles can't quench the thirst in our souls. They can provide insights into our condition (so share them as well), but only Jesus can release us from the power and penalty and pain of our sin and our wounds.

At the same time, remember that preaching information alone will not bring healing into the deepest places of our heart. Trauma specialist Babbette Rothchild has a simple maxim for helping the traumatized: "Trauma trumps rational thought." She's referring to some basic realities of the human brain, a brain that God designed, by the way. Some reactions to trauma are not rooted in the rational systems of our brain. In other words, we can't just preach on God's peace and then insist that trauma victims stop having flashbacks or hyper-arousal. Sometimes the pain and memories are locked and frozen in a different part of the brain. So keep teaching God's truth, but realize that preaching and teaching are only one level in the healing process.

Small Groups

Small groups can and should be the place where we process the information about the Christian life and practice the biblical "one anothers." It's tough to listen to someone's story in a group of fifteen hundred or even fifty. But hopefully groups of six to twelve can provide a safe place to start healing from traumatic life events. My friend Steve the trauma counselor reminds me that small groups should be the place to normalize trauma and brokenness. In these groups we can create safe places for all of us to confess and receive support and prayer for our stories of brokenness. We need to train our small group leaders to expect and facilitate and prayerfully deal with these stories of trauma.

On the other hand, our small group leaders also need to be trained in the gentle art of referral. Most ordinary small groups are not therapy groups. That would stretch a group to the breaking point. So, as the stories of pain and trauma come forth, small group leaders may need to gently say, "Bill, we love you and we will be here for you, but you also need to share your story with a trained counselor who can help you process this. We will walk beside you. We're not leaving you; we're just asking you to take your healing to the next level." This is a delicate and difficult calling, but with a little training and wisdom and winsomeness, most small groups can encourage this process of healing.

Worship

Worship can be a powerful way to heal the traumatized. Worship leaders can study and reflect on songs and passages that bring us into the healing presence of the cross of Jesus. Laments can be spoken, sung, and recited. Every time we gather around the Lord's Table and say the words, "This is my body, broken for you," we remember and celebrate that we know a traumatized God. The Lord's Supper or a sermon can be followed by quiet singing and an invitation for people to slip out and receive prayer for past traumatic experiences.

Patience

Finally, be patient with the process of healing. How do we love people who don't change right away? Part of the answer is this: we display patience and forbearance (see Col. 3:12–14 and Eph. 4:2). Patience is the grease that lubricates close Christian relationships. Out of love, we accept that the journey of spiritual change is long and slow and people often get stuck—but we keep loving people anyway. Of course, as I remember and reflect on God's infinite patience with me, a broken sinner before a holy God, it makes it easy for me to offer a taste of God's patience with other fellow strugglers.

Putting the Pieces Together

A Practical Guide for Your Journey of Healing

(NORMAN WRIGHT)

This chapter on trauma is basic and overly simplified. The information is meant to help you put all the pieces together as you begin and continue your journey of healing after traumatic life events. If you identify yourself as one of those experiencing any degree of post-traumatic stress disorder (PTSD) or you know someone who fits the characteristics, remember this:

1. *Being traumatized is not incurable. Recovery is possible,* but it is a slow process.
2. *You will need to work with a professional,* someone who is equipped to assist those experiencing trauma. This could include a highly trained minister, chaplain, or therapist.

3. *You can promote healing through understanding.* The more you learn about trauma for yourself or for others, the more you will feel in control of your life.

There is another side to trauma. The current research on those traumatized indicates the majority of victims say they eventually benefited from the trauma in some way. And these are people who experienced as much pain as those who didn't fully recover. How did they benefit? There was a change of values, a greater appreciation for life, a deepening of spiritual beliefs, a feeling of greater strength and appreciation and building relationships.

The most important element in recovering is to remain connected to other people.[1]

After conducting extensive research on those suffering with PTSD, Aphrodite Matsakis has taken a positive approach to the healing process. She explains that for healing to occur you need to stop seeing yourself as a person who is diseased or deficient. Don't refer to yourself as a traumatized person. You are not abnormal because of your trauma symptoms: it is the event or events that you experienced that are abnormal. The event was so out of the ordinary that it overwhelmed you, as it would anyone.[2]

There are three stages in trauma recovery: the *cognitive* stage, the *emotional* stage, and the *mastery* stage. The cognitive or thinking stage involves fully facing your trauma, remembering it, and even reconstructing it mentally. This isn't a matter of dwelling in the past, but of taking fragmented and disconnected memories and pulling them together so that you can make sense of the present. Sometimes this stage involves talking with others, re-creating the scene, or reading written accounts of it. When this is accomplished, you will then be able to view what happened from a new perspective—an objective view rather than a judgmental view.[3]

In the cognitive stage you need to look at what happened to you as a detached observer (even though it may be difficult) rather than as an emotionally involved participant. If you're able to work through this stage, you will acquire a new assessment of what your real choices were during your traumatic experience. You will have a better understanding of how the event has impacted the totality of your life, and you will be able to reduce the self-blame that most of us experience. Finally, you will gain a clearer understanding of who or what you are angry at.

The cognitive stage deals with the mental area, but healing and recovery must also involve the emotional level. This second stage will necessitate dealing with any of the feelings you repressed in any way because of the trauma. You must experience those emotions at the gut level. This can be difficult, because many people have a fear of feeling even worse and losing control. You don't have to act on the feelings, nor will they take over your life. But you do need to face them. These emotions could include anger, anxiety, grief, fear, sadness—the list goes on and on.

The final stage is the mastery stage. This is when you find new meaning through what you have experienced; your perspective becomes that of a survivor rather than a victim. A person who has a relationship with Jesus Christ and a biblical worldview has a greater potential to become a survivor.

Mastering the trauma involves making your own decisions instead of allowing experiences, memories, or other people to make decisions for you. This is a time of growth, change, and new direction in your life. What you learn because of a trauma, you probably could not have learned any other way. Look at what Scripture says about this:

> Blessed be the God and Father of our Lord Jesus Christ, the Father of mercies and God of all comfort; who comforts us in all our affliction so that we will be able to comfort those who are in any affliction with the comfort with which we ourselves are comforted by God. For just as the sufferings of Christ are ours in abundance, so also our comfort is abundant through Christ. But

if we are afflicted, it is for your comfort and salvation; or if we are comforted, it is for your comfort, which is effective in the patient enduring of the same sufferings which we also suffer.

2 Corinthians 1:3–6 NASB

I've had people ask me, "How do I know I'm growing and getting better?" First, you have to develop a new way of looking at progress. It may be slow. There may be regressions. You need to focus on the improvements rather than the times you feel stuck. One man told me that he rated his progress each month on a scale of one to ten, as well as his entire journey of healing up to that point. That helped him understand his own progress.

How can you tell if you're progressing and moving ahead? Your symptoms become less frequent, and the fear you struggled with will become less intense. The disheartening fear of going crazy or insane will also diminish.

Taking positive steps like this will help you make the shift from victim to survivor. *Believing* that you can become a survivor will accelerate this process.

As you move through your journey to recovery, the rigidity that helps you cope will diminish. You *will* gradually discover the value of flexibility and spontaneity to the degree that you are comfortable with it, based on your own unique personality type.

One of the delights of recovery is developing a new appreciation of life. You begin to see what you weren't seeing before, to hear what you couldn't hear before, to taste what was tasteless before.

Some people rediscover their sense of humor and all its healing properties.

You *will* discover a new and deeper sense of empathy for the wounded around you. You actually become a wounded healer and have greater compassion for others.

Romans 12:15, which says, "Weep with those who weep," takes on a new meaning.[4]

Because those who are recovering commonly struggle to see and measure their progress, I've had people keep a daily or weekly journal in which they explicitly write out what they are experiencing or feeling. Some keep a time line of recovery. Some do both. Over time this makes a person aware, in a tangible way, of his or her recovery.

Let's consider some steps you can take for your recovery.

Perhaps you're like many individuals. You've been avoiding the trauma in your life. You could even be quite skilled in sidestepping visiting the event(s), as many are. Or it could be that there is a conscious fixation on what occurred in your life. Some I've talked to say it's like a free-floating aberration just under their conscious memory that makes a number of forays into their conscious mind each day. It comes and goes and comes and goes.

Wherever you are and whatever the event, if you were to come to me for help, let me tell you what I would *not* do. I wouldn't ask you about your trauma—what it was, where or when it happened, or how it was affecting you. This is not what some expect. All of what I wouldn't ask at first is important. But for you to move forward with your life, your entire story needs to be reconstructed. And this is what I *would* do—ask you to tell me about your life before the event and the circumstances that led up to it. I'd like to know about your relationships, ideals, dreams, conflicts, interests, and struggles prior to your trauma. Many tend to forget they had a life before the trauma, and this can help you put it in perspective. You could do this with a counselor or a trusted and sensitive friend, or you could write it in detail yourself, first asking Jesus to be present with you as you write. And when you write, don't use a computer but write in longhand.

Some of your previous life you may want to revisit and some you may not. But it's helpful for you to develop a continuity with your past.

When you've experienced trauma, sometimes that's all you remember. So if you are able to leapfrog over that event back to what your life was like before the trauma, you can *look at your life as it was*. What was your life like? What did you do each day? Answer the following questions to help you remember your life before the trauma:

- What was your biggest struggle then?
- What fulfilled you?
- What did you enjoy the most?
- What did you look like then? (It helps to be very specific about this. Sometimes pictures and videos help the process.)
- Who were your friends?
- What did you like and not like about yourself?
- Who did you get along with?
- Who didn't you get along with?
- What did you believe about God then?
- What were your Christian practices, such as prayer?
- What were your beliefs about life then?
- What were you realistic about? Naïve about?
- What did you want out of life then?
- What were your goals or dreams for yourself then?
- What are your goals or dreams for yourself now?
- What would you like to be different now?

As you look at what you write, what specifically is different now? What alternatives can you come up with to make your life more the way you want it to be? Make a list of all the things you would like to happen now (dream big), and then check off what possibly could happen if you choose to pursue this avenue. What would keep you from growing and changing? For many, it's the lack of a plan. Dreams can fade without a plan. Perhaps someone else could help you with this part of the exercise.

Overcoming trauma is a process—a journey. But you don't travel the journey alone; the Lord is with you.

> The Spirit of the Sovereign LORD is on me,
>   because the LORD has anointed me
>   to preach good news to the poor.
> He has sent me to bind up the brokenhearted,
>   to proclaim freedom for the captives
>   and release for the prisoners.
>
> Isaiah 61:1

Your next step is to reconstruct the traumatic event in a factual way. For some this will be extremely difficult to do alone because of what occurred and will necessitate the presence of a trained therapist. Others will find the writing to be part of the healing for them. Writing in this way can bring the fragments of the memories, both those available and those frozen, together so you have an organized and detailed narrative. At times you may be at a loss for words at the most painful parts, and if so, draw using pencil or crayons in a realistic or abstract manner. It's important to state not just the facts but to respond as if you're watching a movie. Describe not only what *you* are seeing but what *you* are hearing, smelling, feeling, and what *you* are thinking.

Your reaction to what you have written may be mixed. You may want to reject and discard it. You may want to rewrite it again and again to fill in the gaps, or you may feel you've overdone it and written a book. The goal is to get every bit of it out of you and onto the paper.

If this experience is overwhelming, you may need to work at it in pieces and put it aside at times. And yet healing comes through the process of facing the pain and reconstructing the story.[5]

When this part is complete, you will have more control of your life. When intrusive thoughts or memories or sensations come back into your life, you can say to them, "Well, welcome. I've experienced and faced you before. You have a purpose. And I won't forget you or the story even when you're absent. I have everything in writing so I won't forget. You can remain or go—whatever you choose is all right since I'm moving on with my life." I have listened to statements like this from counselees, and when stated, it's apparent the person has moved from the posture of victim to an overcomer.

Often the reconstruction of the story can make you more aware of what you've lost, which may put you into a deeper sense of mourning. But this is an opportunity for recovery.

The next step is perhaps best thought of as an evaluation of how the trauma has impacted your life. How did this event change you? Challenge you? What did it do to your values and beliefs? How did this event affect your relationships?

One of the purposes of telling and retelling your trauma story is to lessen the intense feelings and eventually see it fade like other memories. It no longer is as significant as it was, and you no longer refer to yourself as a traumatized person.[6]

It's important to continue writing. And now it's no longer about the past but your future—what you want it to be and who you want to be. It's time to reconnect with life. Old beliefs, ways of responding, and a new outlook can be developed to replace the discards. The exaggerated responses can move to a balanced level. Each new step and success needs to be reinforced, not so much by others, but by you. It's learning the phrase, "I can do this."

As you write, take the time to write *a future report on yourself in three years.* Describe what you really want to be like in three years. What will it take for you to arrive? At first you may not believe it's possible. That's all right. Rely on others' encouragement and belief in you. And above all, rely on God's belief in who you are and what you're capable of doing. Our heavenly Father is a God who knows how to turn your mourning and your fear into joy! And where you see hopelessness, he sees hope, and where you see loss, he sees gain. You are so highly valued by God that it's difficult to grasp.

A few years ago the choir at our church sang an anthem based on Zephaniah 3:17. I had never heard the song before. The words were printed in our church bulletin, and I have read them many times since because they encourage me, inspire me, and remind me of what I mean to God:

> And the Father will dance over you in joy!
> He will take delight in whom He loves.
> Is that a choir I hear singing the praises of God?
> No, the Lord God Himself is exulting over you in song!
> And He will joy over you in song!
> My soul will make its boast in God.
> For He has answered all my cries.
> His faithfulness to me is as sure as the dawn of a new day.
> Awake my soul, and sing!
> Let my spirit rejoice in God!
> Sing, O daughter of Zion, with all of your heart!
> Cast away fear for you have been restored!
> Put on the garment of praise as on a festival day.
> Join with the Father in glorious, jubilant song.
> God rejoices over you in song![7]

As you move forward you will probably find yourself reaching out to help others or even correct injustices. You will find a positive use for what you have experienced. Nothing we have experienced is ever wasted in God's economy.

As you consider moving on with your life there are many factors that influence your recovery process. Part of it is how severely you were traumatized. A major step is to make peace with the memory of what happened to you. The memory that was tucked away needs to be visited and made part of your conscious memory so it can "inform the future rather than foreclosing it."[8]

And the way in which you look at the symptoms of your trauma requires a shift in understanding their meaning. It's a matter of learning to appreciate them and to see them as something even positive. Appreciate these life-preserving resources from a time of extraordinary circumstances in your life.[9] "The healing process begins not with trying to push the symptoms away, but rather with trying to understand and befriend them for the great protection that they have been. The symptoms originate in human resiliency and are not a sign of weakness or failure."[10]

Ordinarily, we know when an event is over, even if it was dangerous and we heave that sigh of relief. But if you've been traumatized, you could be reliving the event as though it's continually occurring in your present life. And this is disruptive. How can you resume the normal course of your life with this interruption? When trauma invades your life, it tends to stop time. It plants a chip in your mind, and even though your life goes on, you're still stuck back at the moment the trauma occurred. And who knows when the trauma will appear on the scene again?

When you've been traumatized, you experience traumatic memories, which are unlike ordinary memories, as well as traumatic dreams, which are a far cry from your typical dreams. These dreams share many of the unusual features of the traumatic memories you experience when you're awake. They could be exact replicas of the traumatic event or a variation. And they could be repeated. The feeling is they're occurring right now in the present and they're terrifying. They seem all too real. These dreams can also occur in stages of our sleep in which we don't usually dream. And when you've been traumatized, you can not only relive your trauma in thoughts and dreams but in your actions as well.[11]

As we've already mentioned in chapter 6, *dissociation* is a key word connected with trauma. It's one of the most common responses to a traumatic situation. It's also a common occurrence for all of us in our everyday life. Have you ever sat through a boring lecture and your mind wandered to other places and thoughts? All of a sudden your mind returned to the lecture and you realized that you missed the last fifteen minutes. That's dissociation. Or have you ever taken a trip, driving for several hours, and upon arrival at your destination you have no memory of several segments of the trip? That's dissociation. Our interstate highway system was deliberately constructed with occasional curves to keep us from falling into a trance state described as "highway hypnosis." Dissociation is when your body is present but your mind is somewhere else. You daydream—so do I. We engage in this during a sermon, a required meeting, or a conflict that we're engaged in without any apparent resolution possible.

In trauma, dissociation means emotional and mental escape when physical escape isn't possible. It's a process of not allowing the painful situation into our conscious awareness. Another means is to block its emotional impact by mentally or emotionally compartmentalizing the trauma. Your mind walls off the trauma experience similar to the way your body attempts to wall off an infection. And it's most likely to take place if your trauma was severe or repeated, or if it occurred at an early age. This allows you to detach and avoid the impact of the trauma. We mentally go away.

Dissociation blunts or obliterates the reality of the trauma while it is in progress. It dulls it. And second, it blocks our memory so it prevents repetitive flashbacks. It is a splitting off of a personality or personality state that holds the memory of the trauma. It cuts out a piece of life and puts it out of sight and out of mind. This enables the personality state that has forgotten the trauma to go on with life as if nothing has happened.

It's common to lose track of time while dissociating. It's also possible to block off some parts of your experience and not others.

189

Avoiding the pain of trauma is a normal response, but there's a cost to dissociation. Dissociating the trauma also takes it out of the main stream of memories. It's not connected to the others—it exists in isolation—and it's not very stable even there. It stays just under the surface like a partially filled volleyball, and every now and then the experience, with all its baggage, pops to the surface unannounced, unexpected, and unwelcome. It's an intruder. It's not part of the long-term memory system, nor is it connected to present awareness. And when it bursts through, you end up not feeling like yourself.

When you keep feelings and memories from yourself, it interferes with your relationship with yourself. This can hinder you from enjoying time spent alone or feeling okay about yourself or being able to handle strong feelings. The numbness that dissociation brings not only shuts off negative feelings but also most, if not all, positive feelings. You end up with limitations. But if you make a choice to gradually open the door and face what you fear, you not only engage the painful feelings but the positive ones as well.

If you were traumatized and used dissociation, you didn't plan it or consciously choose it to begin with. It was your survival instinct that took over. But now you have another choice. You can consciously choose or plan to use dissociation at this time. This thought may be foreign to you, but it's both possible and useful. If you're frightened, you may be able to reduce your fear at this time by withdrawing to a safer place in your mind. If you're in charge of the dissociation, it may be helpful. I've done this during the unpleasant part of a doctor's exam or a shot or when the dentist is drilling, and perhaps you have too.[12] But don't use it to avoid unpleasant feelings. These do need to be visited gradually, exposed, faced, and released.

Two of the symptoms of trauma are intrusive memories and flashbacks. Intrusive memories are like a fragment of a song that plays again and again, the annoying tune that you cannot get out of your head until its distraction has run its course. These memories, however, are much more disturbing.

It is confusing to experience intrusive memories because of the lack of connection between the material in the memory and when and how it appears. The memory intrudes without its context, like the recollection of a past loss mysteriously pressing into consciousness during a pleasant meal.

Unlike intrusive memories, which carry some understanding that what is coming to mind is a past event, people experiencing flashbacks are temporarily living in the moment of the trauma with all the attending physical anguish.

Flashbacks of trauma evoke the original sense of terror and helplessness. Flashbacks are a function of memory presented in such a way that the material of the past is the agony of the present. But it's also a way your brain is attempting to heal yourself—it's your mind's way of attempting to make sense of what happened. Both flashbacks and intrusive memories are the reality of the wound breaking through into your conscious mind.[13]

Transforming trauma is movement from the desire to inflict violence on others through retribution—to those who have hurt us or to ourselves for not having responded differently—to a reclamation of voice, hope, and imagination. It is impossible to make that transition without spirituality—a belief in something more than what is currently seen or understood. In particular, the Good News of Jesus Christ invites us to walk with a risen Savior who can let his light shine even through our cracks and wounds. He can turn our scars into alleluias.

Dr. Rachael Naomi Remen shares a powerful story of a young man whose cracks became the source of light and beauty. The young man found his identity in his athletic abilities. So after he was diagnosed with osteogenic sarcoma and the doctors amputated his right leg below the knee, he was devastated. Remen claims that he consistently exhibited the most anger she had ever seen in one of her patients. He spewed anger and hatred on well people. In her second meeting with the young man, Remen asked him to take a box of crayons and draw a picture of his body. He quickly took a black crayon and drew a crude vase with an ugly crack running down the middle of the vase. Remen commented, "It seemed to me that the drawing was a powerful statement of his pain and the finality of his loss. It was clear that this broken vase could never hold water, could never function as a vase again."[14]

But in time, ever so slowly, his anger began to shift and even fade. The once rage-filled young man actually started to affect other young people on the surgical ward whose problems were similar to his own. Due to his own wounds, he was able to help and offer encouragement when no one else could. Eventually he also started ministering to the parents and families of cancer patients. The doctors referred more and more patients to him as the young man's rage turned to joy and love.

Dr. Remen concludes the story by describing their last meeting:

> I opened his chart and found the picture of the broken vase that he had drawn two years before. Unfolding it, I asked him if he remembered the drawing he had made of his body. He took it in his hands and looked at it for the first time. "You know," he said, "it's really not finished." Surprised, I extended my basket of crayons toward him. Taking a yellow crayon, he began to draw lines radiating from the crack in the vase to the very edges of the paper. Thick yellow lines. I watched, puzzled. He was smiling. Finally he put his finger on the crack, looked at me, and said softly, "This is where the light comes through."[15]

As the apostle Paul witnessed, the light of Jesus shines into the world through our cracks and our wounds (2 Cor. 4:6). Trauma disrupts and ruptures our previous understanding of life. Our journey toward healing requires a new vision that both knows the depth of the wound and has witnessed the possibility for hope.[16]

I have three other suggestions for you. Find a qualified Christian therapist to work with you and your trauma. Second, get a copy of *The Post-Traumatic Stress Disorder Sourcebook* by Dr. Glenn R. Schiraldi, one of the most helpful resources I have found. Third, don't abandon your faith but renew it. It will change. It will be tested. Listen to the words of Dr. Diane Langberg:

> What does trauma do to faith? There are two things to keep in mind. The first is that trauma freezes thinking. Someone who has experienced trauma thinks about herself, her life, her relationships, and her future through the grid of the trauma. Trauma stops growth because it shuts everything down. It is of the nature of death. The thinking that grows out of the traumatic experience controls the input from the new experience. People who went to work every day in the World Trade Center and never thought about safety in the building or cared what floor they worked on will ponder such things daily. Some will decide to take a job or not based on what floor it is on. It will not matter that the vast majority of tall buildings in the world remain standing. The trauma will serve as the grid.
>
> Second, we learn about the unseen through the seen. We are of the earth, earthy. God teaches us truths through the world around us. We grasp a bit of eternity by looking at the sea. We get a glimmer of infinity by staring into space. We learn about the shortness of time by the quickness of a vapor. Jesus taught this way. He said he was bread, light, water and the vine. We look at the seen and learn about the unseen. Consider the sacraments—water, bread, and wine. We are taught about the holiest of all through the diet of a peasant. This method of pointing to the seen to teach about the unseen is used by God in teaching us about his character.
>
> Many who suffered through intense trauma will struggle with the same two seemingly irreconcilable realities: God who is a refuge and trauma. Each seems to cancel out the other, yet both exist. The human mind can manage either alternative—trauma and no

God, or God and no trauma. What is one to do with trauma *and* God?

The only answer to this dilemma is the cross of Jesus Christ, for it is there that trauma and God come together. The components of trauma such as fear, helplessness, destruction, alienation, silence, loss and hell have all been endured by Christ. He understands trauma. He willingly entered into trauma for us. He endured trauma, abandoned by the Father so that we never have to be traumatized without the presence of the Father.

Jesus came in the flesh, explaining God to us. Jesus brought the unseen down into flesh-and-blood realities.

The cross demonstrates the extent of the love of God. The cross covers the failures of the suffering. The cross of Christ is God with us in our grief, our suffering, our trauma and our sorrows. We serve and worship a traumatized Savior.[17]

Remember, the last chapter of your trauma hasn't been written yet. And you can write that chapter. With God's help and presence you can survive the storms of trauma.

Notes

Chapter 1 When Trauma Hits Home

1. Bruce D. Perry and Maia Szalavitz, *The Boy Who Was Raised as a Dog: And Other Stories from a Child Psychiatrist's Notebook* (New York: Basic Books, 2006), 231–32.

Chapter 2 What Is Trauma?

1. Christine Armario, "Brutal Attack, Unsolved Mystery," *Newsday*, August 1, 2007, A4–A5.

2. Don Meichenbaum, *A Clinical Handbook/Practical Therapist Manual for Assessing and Treating Adults with Post-Traumatic Stress Disorder (PTSD)* (Waterloo, Ontario: Institute Press, 1995), adapted, 510–11.

3. Aphrodite Matsakis, *I Can't Get Over It! A Handbook for Trauma Survivors* (Oakland, CA: New Harbinger, 1992), adapted, 6–7.

4. Elie Wiesel, *Parade Magazine, Los Angeles Times*, October 2001, 4–5.

5. Lewis Smedes, *How Can It Be All Right When Everything Is All Wrong?* (San Francisco: Harper & Row, 1982), 55–56.

6. Judith Herman, *Trauma and Recovery: The Aftermath of Violence—from Domestic Abuse to Political Terror* (New York: Basic Books, 1992), 35.

7. Matsakis, *I Can't Get Over It!* adapted, 18–22.

8. Raymond B. Flannery Jr., *Post-Traumatic Stress Disorder* (New York: Crossroad, 1992), adapted, 36–37.

9. Herman, *Trauma and Recovery*, 37.

10. Robert Hicks, *Failure to Scream* (Nashville: Nelson, 1993), 46.

Notes

Chapter 3 The Emotions of Trauma: Anger

1. Matsakis, *I Can't Get Over It!* 170.
2. Ibid., adapted, 195.
3. Teresa Rhodes McGee, *Transforming Trauma* (Maryknoll, NY: Orbis Books, 2005), adapted, 100–104.
4. Glenn R. Schiraldi, *The Post-Traumatic Stress Disorder Sourcebook* (San Francisco: McGraw-Hill, 2000), 125.
5. McGee, *Transforming Trauma*, 104–5.
6. Information has been adapted from the following articles: "New Hope, New Dreams" by Roger Rosenblatt, *Time*, August 26, 1996, v. 148, N10, p. 40 (13); Fighting to Fund an 'Absolute Necessity'" by Kendall Hamilton, *Newsweek*, July 1, 1996, v. 128, N1, p. 56 (1); "We Draw Strength from Each Other" by Liz Smith, *Good Housekeeping*, June 1996, v. 322, N6, p. 86 (5).
7. Matsakis, *I Can't Get Over It!* adapted, 175.
8. Schiraldi, *Post-Traumatic Stress Disorder Sourcebook*, adapted, 126–27.

Chapter 4 The Emotions of Trauma: Guilt, Fear, and Depression

1. Carol Staudacher, *Beyond Grief: A Guide for Recovering from the Death of a Loved One* (Oakland, CA: New Harbinger, 1987), adapted, 10–31.
2. Earl A. Grolman, *Living When a Loved One Has Died* (Boston: Beacon, 1987), 39–41.
3. Shirley Inrau, "Learning with a Dying Mother," *Confident Living*, December 1987, 20–22.
4. Maggie Scarf, *Unfinished Business: Pressure Points in the Lives of Women* (New York: Doubleday, 1985), 85–87.
5. Brenda Poinsett, *Why Do I Feel This Way?* (Colorado Springs: NavPress, 1996), 131–32.
6. Schiraldi, *Post-Traumatic Stress Disorder Sourcebook*, 142.
7. David W. Willske, *Gone, but Not Lost* (Grand Rapids: Baker, 1992), 55.

Chapter 5 The Emotions of Trauma: Grief

1. Nicholas Wolterstorff, *Lament for a Son* (Grand Rapids: Eerdmans, 1987), 33.
2. Margaret Braunley, *Grieving God's Way* (Enumclaw, WA: WinePress, 2004), 133.
3. Gerald Sittser, *A Grace Disguised* (Grand Rapids: Zondervan, 1996), 47.
4. Ken Gire, *The Weathering Grace of God: The Beauty God Brings from Life's Upheavals* (Ann Arbor, MI: Servant, 2001), 69.
5. Joanne T. Jozefowski, *The Phoenix Phenomenon: Rising from the Ashes of Grief* (Northvale, NJ: Jason Aronson), 17.
6. Harry and Cheryl Salem, *From Grief to Glory* (New Kennsington, PA: Whitaker House, 2003), 89.
7. Nancy Guthrie, *Holding On to Hope: A Pathway through Suffering to the Heart of God* (Wheaton: Tyndale, 2002), 11–12.

8. Judy Tatelbaum, *The Courage to Grieve* (New York: HarperPerennial, 1980), 15.

9. Glen W. Davidson, *Understanding Mourning* (Minneapolis: Augsburg, 1984), adapted, 24–27.

10. Bob Diets, *Life after Loss* (Tucson, AZ: Fisher, 1988), adapted, 126–33.

11. Joyce Rupp, *Praying Our Goodbyes* (New York: Ivy, 1988), adapted, 94–97.

12. Ibid., 7–8.

Chapter 6 Telling Your Story

1. Diane Langberg, *Counseling Survivors of Sexual Abuse* (Wheaton: Tyndale, 1997), 55.

2. Brooks Brown, "Columbine Survivor with Words for Virginia Students," *All Things Considered*, NPR, airdate April 18, 2007.

3. Aphrodite Matsakis, *Trust after Trauma: A Guide to Relationships for Survivors and Those Who Love Them* (Oakland, CA: New Harbinger, 1998), 272.

4. "Can Sharing Stories Help People Heal from Tragedy?" *Talk of the Nation*, NPR, August 22, 2006.

5. Perry and Szalavitz, *The Boy Who Was Raised and a Dog*, 165.

6. Ibid.

Chapter 7 Finding God after Trauma

1. Herman, *Trauma and Recovery*, 178.

2. Kevin Coughlin, "We Don't Leave Our Wounded on the Battlefield: Recognizing the Potential for Chaplaincy in Post-Traumatic Treatment," http://www.vietnamveteranministers.org/coughlin_paper.htm.

3. Margaret Nelson-Pechota, *Spirituality and PTSD in Vietnam Combat Veterans*, http://www.vietnamveteranministers.org/spirituality_intro.htm.

4. C. S. Lewis, *A Grief Observed* (London: Faber and Faber, 1961), 9.

5. The same Hebrew word is used in Deuteronomy 32:11 to describe the fluttering of a mother eagle stirring its young to flight.

6. Os Guinness, *Unspeakable: Facing Up to Evil in an Age of Genocide and Terror* (San Francisco: HarperSanFrancisco, 2005), 140.

7. Ibid., 145.

8. John Stott, *The Cross of Christ* (Downers Grove, IL: InterVarsity, 1986), 329.

9. Guinness, *Unspeakable*, 137, 145.

10. N. T. Wright, *Evil and the Justice of God* (Downers Grove, IL: InterVarsity, 2006), 14.

11. Wolterstorff, *Lament for a Son*, 85.

12. For more on theophostic prayer, see Edward M. Smith, *Healing Life's Hurts through Theophostic Prayer: Let the Light of Christ Set You Free from Lifelong Fears, Shame, False Guilt, Anxiety and Emotional Pain* (Ventura, CA: Regal Books, 2004).

Notes

13. Tod Bolsinger, "The Place Where Pain and Love Meet," unpublished sermon, January 28, 2007.

14. John Piper, *Future Grace* (Sisters, OR: Multnomah, 1995), 122–23.

Chapter 8 Embracing Your Identity in Christ

1. David Benner, *The Gift of Being Yourself: The Sacred Call to Self-Discovery* (Downers Grove, IL: InterVarsity, 2005), 49.

2. Matsakis, *Trust after Trauma*, 29.

3. Jean Vanier, *From Brokenness to Community* (New York: Paulist, 1992), 13.

4. William Faulkner, "A Rose for Emily," in *Collected Stories* (New York: Vintage, 1995), 124.

5. Benner, *Gift of Being Yourself*, 49.

6. According to trauma expert Aphrodite Matsakis, trauma often throws us into situations "where all the choices available are unacceptable or involve a violation of personal ethics. Usually, no matter what choice you make, you must betray yourself, or an important value. . . . But with trauma, there might not be a way to make amends, because some of the losses are irreversible" (*Trust after Trauma*, 166).

7. Romano Guardini, *The Virtues* (Chicago: Regnery, 1967), 34–35.

8. Martin Laird, *Into the Silent Land: A Guide to the Christian Practice of Contemplation* (New York: Oxford University Press, 2006), 120.

Chapter 9 Healing for Children after Trauma

1. John W. James and Russell Friedman, *When Children Grieve* (New York: HarperCollins, 2001), 5.

2. J. William Worden, *Children and Grief: When a Parent Dies* (New York: Guilford, 1996), adapted, 134.

3. Wendy N. Zubenko and Joseph Capozzoli, eds., *Children and Disasters: A Practical Guide to Healing and Recovery* (New York: Oxford University Press, 2002), adapted, 99.

4. Debra Whiting Alexander, *Children Changed by Trauma* (Oakland, CA: New Harbinger, 1999), 5.

5. Ibid., adapted, 96.

6. Dave Ziegler, *Trauma Experience and the Brain* (Phoenix: Acacia, 2002), adapted, 58.

7. Alexander, *Children Changed by Trauma*, adapted, 35.

8. Ziegler, *Trauma Experience*, adapted, 42–44.

9. Ibid., adapted, 56.

10. Robine Karr-Morse and Meridith S. Wiley, *Ghosts from the Nursery: Tracing the Roots of Violence* (New York: Atlantic Monthly, 1997), adapted, 159, 163.

11. Kendall Johnson, *Trauma in the Lives of Children* (Alameda, CA: Hunter House, 1998), adapted, 46–47.

12. Ibid., adapted, 63.

13. Ibid., adapted, 67–72.

6. Dave Ziegler,

14. Ibid., adapted, 99–100.
15. Alexander, *Children Changed by Trauma*, adapted, 81–82.
16. Ibid., 25–26.
17. Ibid., adapted, 196–97.
18. Ibid., adapted, 6.
19. Zubenko and Capozzoli, *Children and Disasters*, 96–97.

Chapter 10 Becoming a Healing Church

1. Herman, *Trauma and Recovery*, 134.
2. Matsakis, *Trust after Trauma*, 36.
3. Ibid.
4. Ibid., 36–39.
5. Quoted in Leanne Van Dyk, ed., *A More Profound Alleluia: Theology and Worship in Harmony* (Grand Rapids: Eerdmans, 2005), 33.
6. Michael Card, *A Sacred Sorrow: Reaching Out to God in the Lost Language of Lament* (Colorado Springs: NavPress, 2005), 29.
7. Judy Hill, "Healing the Wounds of Trauma—Working with Church Leaders," http://www.worldevangelicals.org/commissions/mc/mc_southafrica/resources/Hill%20-%20Healing%20the%20wounds%20of%20trauma.pdf. Accessed February 18, 2008.
8. Denis Haack, "What Does Winsome Look Like? (Part 2)," *Critique* 9 (2001): 10.
9. Herman, *Trauma and Recovery*, 1.
10. Ibid., 70.

Chapter 11 Putting the Pieces Together

1. Terence Mcaunaney, "For Most Trauma Victims Life Is More Meaningful," *Los Angeles Times*, October 7, 2001, 9. Citing research from Richard Tedeschi, University of North Carolina; Dr. Robert Ursuce, Uniformed Services University of the Health Sciences in Bethesda, MD; Dr. Sandra Bloom, the Sanctuary Institute.
2. Matsakis, *I Can't Get Over It!* adapted, 134.
3. Ibid., 15, 153.
4. Ibid., 236.
5. Herman, *Trauma and Recovery*, adapted, 177.
6. Ibid., adapted, 178.
7. "And the Father Will Dance." Lyrics adapted from Zephaniah 3:14, 17 and Psalm 54:2, 4. Arranged by Mark Hayes.
8. McGee, *Transforming Trauma*, 36.
9. Ibid., adapted, 35.
10. Ibid., 36.
11. Herman, *Trauma and Recovery*, adapted, 37–39.
12. Matsakis, *Trust after Trauma*, adapted, 48–49.
13. McGee, *Transforming Trauma*, adapted, 57.

Notes

14. Rachael Naomi Remen, *Kitchen Table Wisdom* (New York: Riverhead, 1996), 115.

15. Ibid., 118.

16. McGee, *Transforming Trauma*, adapted, 17.

17. Diane Mandt Langberg, "Coping with Traumatic Memory," *Marriage & Family: A Christian Journal* 5, no. 4 (2002): 447, 454–55.

Recommended Reading List

David Benner, *The Gift of Being Yourself: The Sacred Call to Self-Discovery* (Downers Grove, IL: InterVarsity, 2005).

David Biebel and Suzanne Foster, *Finding the Way after the Suicide of Someone You Love* (Grand Rapids: Zondervan, 2005).

Michael Card, *A Sacred Sorrow: Reaching Out to God in the Lost Language of Lament* (Colorado Springs: NavPress, 2005).

Susan Duke, *Grieving Forward: Embracing Life after Sudden Loss* (New York: Warner, 2006).

Raymond B. Flannery Jr., *Post-Traumatic Stress Disorder* (New York: Crossroad, 1992).

Earl A. Grolman, *Living When a Loved One Has Died* (Boston: Beacon, 1987).

Os Guinness, *Unspeakable: Facing Up to Evil in an Age of Genocide and Terror* (San Francisco: HarperSanFrancisco, 2005).

Nancy Guthrie, *Holding On to Hope: A Pathway through Suffering to the Heart of God* (Wheaton, IL: Tyndale, 2002).

Judith Herman, *Trauma and Recovery: The Aftermath of Violence—from Domestic Abuse to Political Terror* (New York: Basic Books, 1992).

John W. James and Russell Friedman, *When Children Grieve* (New York: HarperCollins, 2001).

C. S. Lewis, *A Grief Observed* (London: Faber and Faber, 1961).

Aphrodite Matsakis, *I Can't Get Over It! A Handbook for Trauma Survivors* (Oakland, CA: New Harbinger, 1992).

Aphrodite Matsakis, *Trust after Trauma: A Guide to Relationships for Survivors and Those Who Love Them* (Oakland, CA: New Harbinger, 1998).

Teresa Rhodes McGee, *Transforming Trauma* (Maryknoll, NY: Orbis, 2005).

Bruce D. Perry, *The Boy Who Was Raised as a Dog: And Other Stories from a Child Psychiatrist's Notebook* (New York: Basic Books, 2006).

Brenda Poinsett, *Why Do I Feel This Way?* (Colorado Springs: NavPress, 1996).

Glenn R. Schiraldi, PhD, *The Post-Traumatic Stress Disorder Sourcebook* (San Francisco: McGraw-Hill, 2000).

Gerald Sittser, *A Grace Disguised* (Grand Rapids: Zondervan, 1996).

Lewis Smedes, *How Can It Be All Right When Everything Is All Wrong?* (San Francisco: Harper & Row, 1982).

Edward M. Smith, *Healing Life's Hurts through Theophostic Prayer: Let the Light of Christ Set You Free from Lifelong Fears, Shame, False Guilt, Anxiety and Emotional Pain* (New Creation Publishing, 2005).

John Stott, *The Cross of Christ* (Downers Grove, IL, InterVarsity, 1986).

Nicholas Wolterstorff, *Lament for a Son* (Grand Rapids: Eerdmans, 1987).

N. T. Wright, *Evil and the Justice of God* (Downers Grove, IL: InterVarsity, 2006).

Norman Wright and Larry Renetzky, *Healing Grace for Hurting People* (Ventura, CA: Regal, 2007).

Dave Ziegler, PhD, *Trauma Experience and the Brain* (Phoenix, AZ: Acacia, 2002).

Wendy N. Zubenko and Joseph Capozzoli, eds., *Children and Disasters: A Practical Guide to Healing and Recovery* (New York: Oxford University Press, 2002).

H. Norman Wright is a licensed marriage, family, and child therapist, as well as a certified trauma specialist. A graduate of Westmount College, Fuller Theological Seminary, and Pepperdine University, Dr. Wright has received two honorary doctorates from Western Conservative Baptist Seminary and Biola University. He has taught at the graduate level at both Biola University and Talbot Seminary. At the present time, he is research professor of Christian education at Talbot School of Theology.

He is the author of over seventy-five books, including *Helping Those Who Hurt*, *Before You Say I Do*, and *The Handbook of Crisis and Trauma Counseling*. Dr. Wright has pioneered premarital counseling programs throughout the country and conducts seminars on many subjects, including marriage enrichment, parenting, and grief recovery. His current focus is in crisis and trauma counseling and critical incident debriefings within the wider community.

Norm and his wife, Joyce, were married for forty-eight years until her death in 2007. He lives in Bakersfield, California. His hobbies include bass fishing, gardening, and training his golden retriever, Shadow, as a therapy response dog.

Matt Woodley is the senior pastor of Three Village Church on Long Island, an interdenominational, ethnically diverse church family near Stony Brook Prep School and Stony Brook University. He received his MDiv from Theological Seminary. Prior to his ministry on Long Island beginning in 2001, Matt spent thirteen years serving two churches in northern Minnesota. Over the past fifteen years, Matt has been a frequent contributor to various magazines and journals, including *Leadership*, *Discipleship Journal*, the *Mars Hill Review*, and *Rev Magazine*. He is also the author of *Holy Fools* (Tyndale, 2008) and the forthcoming book *Re-imagining Prayer* (InterVarsity Press). Besides pastoring and writing, more than anything else, Matt likes being with his family (Julie and their four children—Bonnie, Mathew, JonMichael, Wesley—and two dogs and two cats). He also loves sitting under "his" apple tree in the local bird sanctuary, drinking coffee and listening to God.

Julie Woodley is the founder and director of Restoring the Heart Ministries (or RTHM), a Christ-centered nonprofit ministry located on Long Island. After finishing a certificate of biblical studies (Bethel Seminary) and a Master's in counseling (Liberty University), Julie started Restoring the Heart Ministries to bring hope and healing to those who have been traumatized by various life hurts. This ministry exists to "run towards" people in deep pain and brokenness. After a ten-year journey, RTHM has produced a cutting-edge, first-class, DVD-based series called *In the Wildflowers*. This unique and powerful series uses real-life stories and the wise words of leading Christian counselors to walk women through a ten-step journey to heal from the wounds of past sexual abuse; future series will address the wounds of post-abortion trauma, general life traumas, and the trauma of cancer. Julie has a part-time private counseling practice that focuses on eating disorders, sexual abuse, depression, and grief and loss. Julie has also spoken extensively around the country to groups. She has co-written a book about her life's story entitled *Restoring the Heart: Experiencing Christ's Healing after Brokenness*. For more information about the RTHM DVD series or Julie's resources or speaking availability, visit www.rthm.cc.

More hope and healing from

DR. NORM WRIGHT

Life is marked by losses—but you can make it through and grow to gain new insights for the journey ahead. *Recovering from Losses in Life* will help you resist the pull toward despair and start on the road back to joy.

www.revellbooks.com